EVERYTHING
C·R·A·F·T·S

Polymer Clay
for Beginners

**Step-by-Step Instructions
for Creating Fun and Original Projects**

Barbara A. McGuire
and Lisa Pavelka

Adams Media
Avon, Massachusetts

An Everything® Series Book.
Everything® and everything.com® are registered trademarks of F+W Publications, Inc.

Published by Adams Media, an F+W Publications Company
57 Littlefield Street, Avon, MA 02322 U.S.A.
www.adamsmedia.com

ISBN: 1-59337-230-2
Printed in the United States of America.

J I H G F E D C B A

Library of Congress Cataloging-in-Publication Data
McGuire, Barbara A.
Everything crafts--polymer clay for beginners / Barbara A. McGuire and Lisa Pavelka.
p.   cm. -- (An everything series book)
ISBN 1-59337-230-2
1. Polymer clay craft. I. Pavelka, Lisa II. Title. III. Everything series.

TT297.M386985 2004
731.4'2--dc22

2004010020

This publication is designed to provide accurate and authoritative information with regard to the subject matter covered. It is sold with the understanding that the publisher is not engaged in rendering legal, accounting, or other professional advice. If legal advice or other expert assistance is required, the services of a competent professional person should be sought.
—From a *Declaration of Principles* jointly adopted by a Committee of the American Bar Association and a Committee of Publishers and Associations

Many of the designations used by manufacturers and sellers to distinguish their products are claimed as trademarks. Where those designations appear in this book and Adams Media was aware of a trademark claim, the designations have been printed with initial capital letters.

This book is available at quantity discounts for bulk purchases.
For information, call 1-800-872-5627.

Some material in this publication has been adapted and compiled
from the following previously published works:

McGuire, Barbara	Creative Stamping in Polymer Clay ©2002 (F+W Publications, Inc.)
Pavelka, Lisa	Polymer Clay Extravaganza ©2002 (F+W Publications, Inc.)
Heaser, Sue	Creative Home Décor in Polymer Clay ©2001 (F+W Publications, Inc.)
Morgan, Stacey	Making Gifts in Polymer Clay ©2001 (F+W Publications, Inc.)

Photography by: Al Parrish and Christine Polomsky. Illustrations by: Fred Fieber at Red Crayola.
Photo Stylists: Jan Nickum, Sharon Sweeney, and Laura Robinson.

Table of Contents

Part I • 1
Polymer Clay 101: The Basics

Part II • 23
Home Sweet Home

Part III • 59
Priceless Jewelry

Part IV • 73
Give the Gift of Clay

Part V • 125
Dress Your Desk!

Welcome to the *Everything® Crafts* Series!

If you want to get in touch with your inner creativity but aren't sure where to begin, you've already completed Step One—choosing the perfect resource to help you get started. The EVERYTHING® CRAFTS books are ideal for beginners because they provide illustrated, step-by-step instruction for creating fun—and unique—projects.

The EVERYTHING® CRAFTS books bring the craft world back to the basics, providing easy-to-follow directions on finding appropriate tools and materials to learn new craft techniques. These clear and readable books guide you every step of the way, from beginning until end, teaching you tips and tricks to get your craft to look just right.

So sit back and enjoy. This experience is all about introducing you to the world of crafts—and, most of all, learning EVERYTHING you can!

A note to our readers:

We are delighted to bring to you over 20 simple, fun, and colorful polymer clay projects! Choose from decorations to gifts, jewelry to desk accessories. There is a little something creative for everyone to take part in with *Everything® Crafts—Polymer Clay for Beginners.*

A very special thanks to Maureen Carlson, Bev Sims, Maria Del Pinto, Audrey and Jimm Freedman, Kim Richards, Donna Kato, Gwen Gibson, Katherine Dewey, Marie Segal, Emi Fukishima, Dotty McMillan, Trina Williams, and Carol Duvall for sharing knowledge of polymer clay. This book would not have been possible if it weren't for the wonderful people of SCD (Society of Craft Designers), the Las Vegas Polymer Clay Guild, and the National Polymer Clay Guild. A special thanks to all of the wonderful and creative people at North Light who made this book come together. And a special thanks to AMACO, Accent Import, All Night Media, American Art Clay Company, Artistic Wire, Beads Plus, Clearsnap, Hampton Art Stamps, Inkadinkadoo, Jacquard Products, Jones Tones, Judikins, Kemper Tools, The Leather Factory, Limited Editions, Manco, The Magnet Source, Polyform Products, Personal Stamp Exchange, Sanford, Scratch Art, Stamp Oasis, Stewart Superior, Timesaver Templates, Toner Plastics, Walnut Hollow, and Welter Stencil for providing many supplies for this book.

—The Editors, EVERYTHING® CRAFTS *Series*

Introduction

Polymer clay is a wonderful treat! It's therapeutic and fascinating! The projects in this book are here for you to expand upon with the techniques as your guide. Try a favorite project with different clay—use different colors, try glitter, make a necklace instead of a bracelet, try the lampshade on a floor lamp, etc. This book should not limit you in using your imagination. You are a beginner and you only start your polymer clay journey here. Do not be afraid to experiment. Simply familiarize yourself with the tools, materials, and precautions in Part I, Polymer Clay 101: The Basics. Once you get acquainted with the clay, the baking, and using your hands and tools, the rest is easy—and fun!

So get going! Dip in! There are too many colors, materials, tools, techniques, projects, and *ideas* to keep waiting! Enjoy.

Polymer Clay 101:
The Basics

Tools & Materials
Unique Techniques

Tools & Materials

Before you begin, it's important that you are prepared with the necessary tools and materials needed to create the projects in this book. For most of you, you probably aren't sure exactly how to be prepared to successfully create the super polymer clay crafts here. Don't worry, everything you need to know and have on hand is in these pages. After that, the materials section at the beginning of each project will alert you to specific colors of clay and tools needed for that specific project. Feel free to mix and match colors and try a few techniques of your own with the projects here. This book is only the beginning of your creative journey. Let's get started!

Terrific Terms and Other Good Stuff to Learn

The following tells you all you need to know about supplies, baking, safety, working with children, and a whole lot more. Use this section to select supplies and to get informed before you start on projects in this book.

Polymer Clay

People have different preferences when it comes to polymer clay. Different people like different clay for different reasons. Why not get a small package of a variety of clays and see which one you like best? The following are brief descriptions of some types of polymer clay.

PREMO! Sculpey

This clay variety is relatively easy to condition, especially if you own a pasta machine. The finished product has a matte finish. PREMO! Sculpey in flesh color is used in the several cartoon-like projects in this book.

Sculpey III

All Sculpey clays are manufactured by Polyform Products of Chicago. This is the clay that most people try first, due to its softness and low price. It is not recommended that you use this type of clay alone for anything that you plan on having around for a while because it breaks very easily.

Transparent Liquid Sculpey

This is a liquid polymer clay that can be tinted with oil paints and used in dozens of different ways. It remains a syrupy liquid until it is baked at the same temperature as regular polymer clay. It is a useful grout for polymer clay mosaics and can simulate delicate enamel effects, stained glass, and ceramic glazes. This clay can also be used as a strong adhesive for attaching fresh clay to baked clay and to fill in cracks.

Granitex

This is stone-effect clay that has tiny fibers mixed into it. Available in a range of subtle colors, this clay has similar properties to Sculpey III and is quite brittle after baking.

FIMO Classic

FIMO clays are manufactured by Eberhard Faber in Germany. Their clay is one of the best-known brands and is available worldwide. Although at times this is the hardest clay to condition, the results are outstanding. This type of clay is great at keeping detail while you continue to work on a piece. It is quite strong once it has been baked.

FIMO Soft

A softer version of FIMO Classic, this type of clay is easy to condition and is available in a range of luscious colors. FIMO Soft and FIMO Classic are often used in projects in this book.

Other Clays

These other clays are manufactured from various places around the globe and are good to become familiar with should you decide not to choose one of the aforementioned brands.

- **Cernit**: manufactured in Germany; colors slightly translucent or porcelain-like; clay not smooth; hand heat causes clay to go limp; baked clay is extremely strong

- **Creall-Therm**: manufactured in the Netherlands; medium-firm clay; lacks more brilliant pigments and metallics; clay is smoothable and strong when baked thoroughly

- **Du-Kit**: manufactured in New Zealand; a medium-firm clay; good for detail; extremely strong after baking and is smoothable

- **Modelene**: manufactured in Australia; has similar properties to Cernit; extremely strong after it has been baked, but not smoothable

- **Modello/Formello**: manufactured in Germany; sold under either of these names; not strong once baked and is not smoothable

Other Materials

Polymer clay can be used in combination with many exciting mediums. You must make sure that the materials being used with the clay are compatible, otherwise you'll be stuck with paint that never dries or pieces that do not age well. The following are a few terrific suggestions that have been tested over the years to dress up your polymer clay creations.

Epoxy Enamel

This is a two-part epoxy resin that can be used to give transparent enamel effects on polymer clay. Some such brands are: Envirotex Lite and Crystal Sheen. Normally used for wood, this deep gloss can be found in hardware or craft materials stores. Enamel paints are not the same.

Varnish

You do not need to varnish baked polymer clay unless you need to protect powders or paint, or unless you want a shiny surface. FIMO matte and gloss spirit- (alcohol) based varnishes are extremely durable. A recommended varnish to use with polymer clay is called Flecto Varathane. Never use solvent-based or acrylic varnish, neither will dry properly on polymer clay.

Tips & Quips: Here are a few notes about polymer clay and food:

- Wash your hands. (See sidebar below.)

- Do not use clay tools for or with food after they have been used with clay.

- Do not eat while working with clay.

- Do not make clay objects that will come in contact with food even after the clay is baked.

- Do not burn the clay.

- Adults should help children and substitute adult tools for age-appropriate tools.

Always Wash Your Hands

Before you work with polymer clay—and after—wash your hands! Although your hands may seem clean, you wouldn't believe the tiny dust particles that end up on the clay if you do not wash your hands directly before working. Make sure you then dry them with a paper towel. You can use the paper towel at your work area to wipe off tools when needed.

After you are done working with the clay, wash your hands again. If there is clay residue left on your hands, it comes off easily with hand sanitizer and a paper towel. Then wash your hands with soap and water.

Cutting Tools

For cutting purposes, a thin blade is best whether your knife is sharp or dull. Soft clay is easy to cut and generally does not require a sharp blade. If you need to slice a thick piece of clay without distorting it, a NuBlade is your best option.

Glue

There are various types of glue you can use when crafting projects with polymer clay. Read below to figure out which glue is best for the projects you want to create (or check out what materials are called for at the start of each project in this book).

Sobo glue

This is a favorite glue that is a personal favorite among many polymer clay artists. A white fabric glue, it is very helpful in attaching clay to porous surfaces, such as wood, paper, and cardboard.

Sobo glue is most commonly applied to the surface of an object and allowed to dry, then the object is covered with clay. The dried glue gives the clay something to grab onto.

Silicone glue

Silicone glue, such as Goop or E-6000, are great for bonding nonporous materials to clay (after the clay has been baked). It is not recommended that children use this kind of adhesive because of harsh fumes. Adults should use this glue only when in a well-ventilated area. When used properly, it is wonderful for holding pin backs, magnets, and button shanks to clay, and it is waterproof too.

Superglue

Occasionally you might want to use superglue. It can attach raw clay to raw clay, raw clay to baked clay, or either of those combinations to porous or nonporous materials. The thing to remember with superglue, other than not to touch it, is that a little goes a long way—so use it sparingly.

Epoxy Glue

This glue shares many of the same qualities as superglue, but the bond is even stronger.

Hot Glue

Hot glue can be tricky. Although it has a strong hold at the start, after a few days or weeks, depending on the brand, whatever was glued together falls apart. This could work to your advantage if you only want a temporary hold, but is not recommended for a permanent bond.

Important Message for Parents

Although the projects in this book are for everyone's enjoyment, please realize that not all of the tools and materials used are suitable for younger children. You are encouraged to work on these projects with your kids and find suitable replacements for adult tools and materials.

Work Surface

If you are working on a surface where you also eat, you should cover the table instead of leaving it unprotected. This will help keep the clay residue and food away from each other. Feel free to work on glass, foam core board, ceramic tiles, countertop or poster board surfaces.

Pasta Machine

Having a pasta machine is not an absolute must, but after using one, you will not know how you ever lived without it. A pasta machine is wonderful for several things, including:

- Creating even, flat sheets of clay in different volumes

- Conditioning and mixing clay

- Rolling clay through with fabric, forcing the clay into the weave of the material

If you do not have a pasta machine, don't worry! The volume measurements for the pasta machine settings are as follows:

Setting 1 = $\frac{1}{8}$"
Setting 2 = $\frac{3}{32}$"
Setting 3 = $\frac{1}{16}$"
Setting 4 = $\frac{3}{64}$"
Setting 5 = $\frac{1}{32}$"

You can also use a brayer, rolling pin, straight water glass, or roller and wooden strips to roll out the clay.

A pasta machine is a great tool when using polymer clay.

More Basic Tools

A few basic materials are needed to complete the projects in this book and are a good starting point to get you set up for polymer clay creations in the future. Any additional items needed are listed at the beginning of each project. When "clay tools" are asked for, it is meant that you have most of the following around your workspace:

- Stylus

- Dull knife

- NuBlade

- Needle tool

- Modeling tools

- Baking sheet (not to be reused for cooking/ eating off of)

- Aluminum foil

- Oven

- Blush makeup

- Small round brush to apply blush and paint

- Blue, black, and white acrylic craft paint

- FIMO Gloss Lacquer

- Sobo white glue

- Toothpicks

- Ruler

- Pin backs

- E-6000 Silicone glue

- Superglue

- Wire

- Wire cutters

Conditioning

All polymer clay needs to be conditioned before you can sculpt with it. (See *Clay Softeners* to learn what you can add to the clay to help condition it following this explanation). Similar to orange juice after it settles, polymer clay needs to be mixed up before it can be used. Some clays are more difficult to condition than others, but the end result is worth it. Here are a few ways to condition the clay:

- Warm the clay before you start. Put the packaged clay in your pocket or sit on it for a while. You can also warm it by setting it on top of a heating pad on a *low* setting. After the clay is warm, take it out of the package and cut it into smaller chunks. Begin pinching and rolling the clay. Soon you will be able to roll and twist the clay until you can bend it without it cracking.

- If you plan to condition a large amount of clay that is a little tougher, such as FIMO Classic, it is strongly suggested that you invest in a food processor. It will make your life much easier! To use a food processor with clay simply chop or slice the clay into smaller pieces and put them into the food processor dish. Try an 8- to 9-ounce amount of clay at a time. Put the lid on and chop the clay for about fifteen seconds. The clay should appear to be in tiny balls. Press them together in a bowl and then dump the clay onto a sheet of aluminum foil. Finish conditioning by twisting and rolling the clay.

- A fantastic conditioned clay combination is three parts FIMO Classic (any color), mixed with one part transparent Sculpey III. The Sculpey III does not change the color of the FIMO clay, but it helps the clay to be more manageable after it has been conditioned.

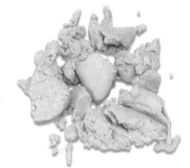

On the left is unconditioned clay; on the right is conditioned clay.

Clay Softeners

FIMO Mix Quick and Sculpey Diluent are softeners that can be added to the clay to condition it. FIMO Mix Quick is a very soft-based color clay and Sculpey Diluent is a liquid softener.

Clay Gun

One very handy tool that you might want to invest in is a clay gun. The clay gun is a metal tube that comes with several disks. Each disk has a different shape in it, and the disks fit into one end of the clay gun while the clay is inserted into the opposite end. A handle which pushes or extracts the clay through the shaped disk is attached. The extracted clay can be used for many things including hair, hay, ropes and strings that need to stay consistent in size. In order to save strain on your hands when using the clay gun, make sure that the clay you use is well conditioned, soft, and warm. It is not absolutely necessary to have a clay gun; it can only help and enhance your projects. Using a clay gun gives you more leverage without adding any strain on your hands.

Storage

The clay will not air dry, and it is a magnet for dust particles, so it is best to store it in a container. Try storing conditioned clay in plastic bags. You can also store clay in glass, metal, and certain types of plastic containers. Don't be alarmed if you store clay in a plastic container and it appears to be melting. Certain plastics chemically react with the plasticizers in the clay, and a different container should be used. It is best to store the clay in a cool, dark place. UV rays can begin to cure clay that is exposed. Likewise, storage next to a heater can affect the clay in the same way.

Measuring

For the projects in this book, use the ruler on the cutting and measuring template for polymer clay. If you do not have or are unable to get one, a plain ruler will work just as well.

When measuring a ball of clay, lay the ball on top of the ruler. Measure by looking down from the top and seeing, which line the very edge of the ball touches. The ball in the photo below is a ½" ball.

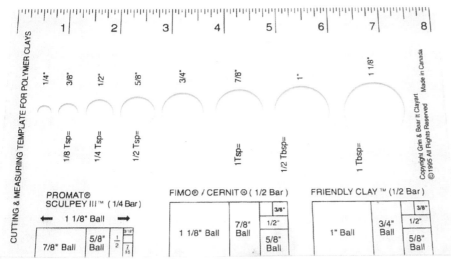

Cutting and measuring template for polymer clay

Measuring a clay ball

Baking

Every polymer clay artist has a preferred method of baking the clay. Some prefer baking clay at 250°F for thirty-five minutes. It is wise to test your oven with an oven thermometer. Some ovens run a bit hot, in which case you should adjust the setting so the thermometer reads 250°F to 255°F. Baking pieces at a lower temperature for a longer period of time helps to keep the colors brighter; sometimes at higher temperatures some clays can darken. Baking at a lower temperature also reduces the risk of burning the clay. Severely burning the clay can result in a release of hazardous fumes, in which case you should ventilate the area and evacuate the room for a while. Do not confuse hazardous fumes with the fumes from regular baking. Regular baking produces a very mild scent. Baking at 250°F to 255°F should not burn any of your pieces.

You can also try using a toaster oven to bake clay. Some toasters can heat up to 300°F and then decrease to 250°F. So if you use one, make sure it's been quite hot and then decreased in temperature before you put your pieces in.

Although many polymer clay artists use toaster ovens, some artists aren't comfortable with the fluctuating temperatures.

Baking Surfaces

Cookie sheets used to bake clay are the ones manufactured with an air space inside. Line the cookie sheet with aluminum foil with the shiny side down. This helps to reduce the chance of spotting on the bottom of the piece. You can also bake with note cards or oven parchment on the cookie sheet. If you bake on something shiny, your piece will have shiny spots left anywhere it touched the shiny surface.

Sealers

Both Polyform Products and FIMO make water-based finishing coats for their clay varieties, and both provide a choice of gloss or matte finish. Some spray glazes are also useful. Krylon acrylic sprays can be used with polymer clay but must be applied very lightly.

Unique Techniques

The following techniques will add to your knowledge about working with polymer clay. Use these techniques to play with the clay or to perfect your skills before you leap to your first official project. Several projects in this book teach you a technique as you create a project, those techniques are millefiori caning and mokume gane.

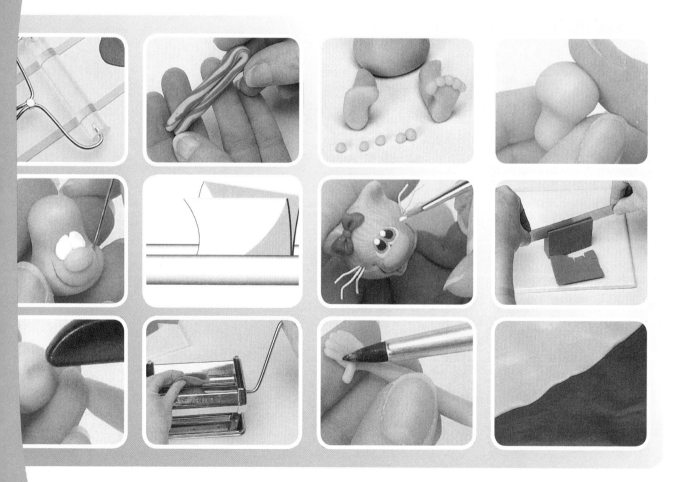

Crafting Clay Characters

Here are instructions and tips for making the basic head, face, arms, hands, legs, and feet used in some of the clay crafts in this book. Master these and you'll be creating clay families in no time!

Head and Face

1 Begin with a ball of flesh-colored clay. The size depends on what you want your character to look like.

2 Position the ball of clay between your finger and thumb. Roll the clay back and forth. The top half should be narrower than the bottom half.

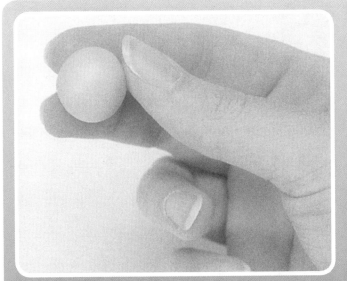

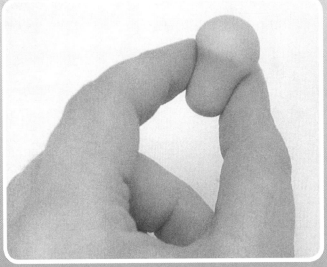

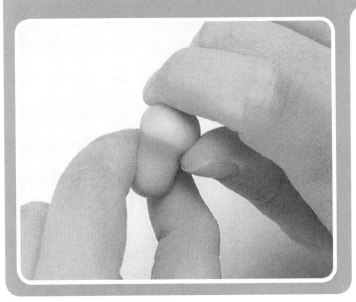

3 Using the side of your thumb, slightly flatten the area just above what should be the cheek line.

4 With the head still upside down, gently bend the face toward the front a little bit.

5 Take a small amount of white clay and use your fingers to shape it into a teardrop. Repeat this to form another teardrop. These are the eyes. Place them side-by-side just above the cheek area.

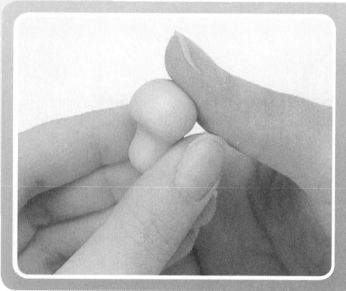

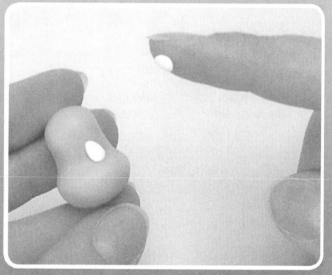

6 Take a small ball of flesh-colored clay. Place it just below the eyes. This is the nose.

7 With a small needle tool, add a smile.

8 Use the end of the stylus to add a finished look to both sides of the smile.

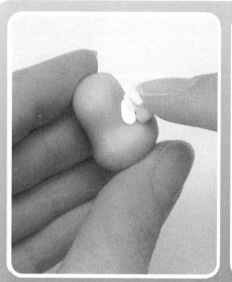

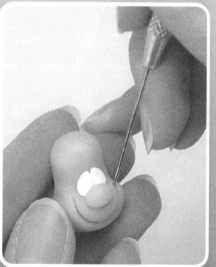

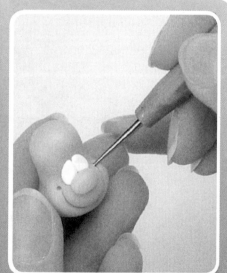

9 If you wish to have an opening in the mouth, insert the stylus and gently pull the clay down.

10 If you have an opening in the mouth, insert a small pink tongue (made from a very tiny amount of pink clay) into the mouth opening with a needle tool.

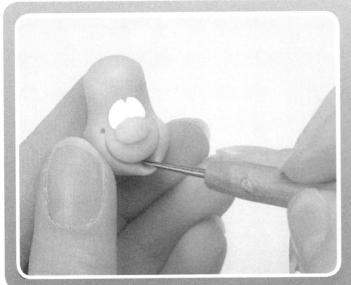

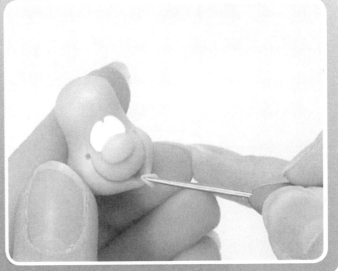

Tips & Quips: The face can be added either before or after the head is attached to the body. This artist adds the face after the head is attached to the body.

11 To make the ears, roll two balls of flesh clay. Hold the first ball to the side of the face. Attach it with the blending tool by inserting it into the center of the ball and pushing the clay into the side of the head. Repeat on the other side.

12 With a small brush add blush to the cheeks and to the top of the nose.

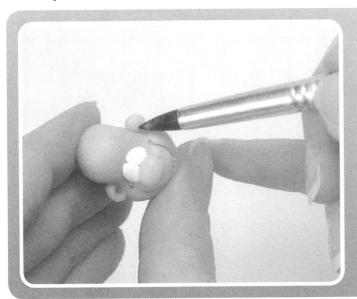

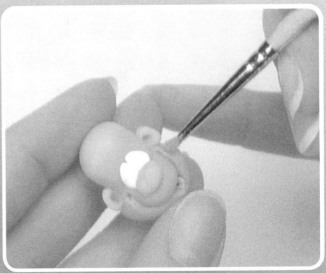

Crafting Clay Characters

Alternate Face

1 A round head instead of the head that was just explained needs an indent for the eyes to lie in or else the eyes will protrude too far from the head. To make the indent, use the handle end of the knife.

2 For the eyes, select the color you want to use for the iris. Use a small, round brush to paint on the color. Use the shape of the eye as a guide, leaving white showing at the bottom.

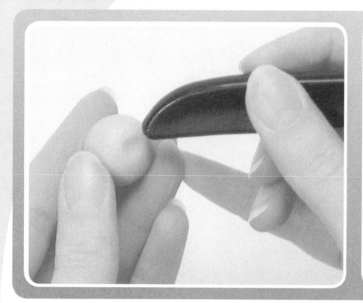

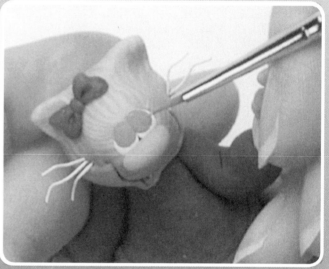

3 Use black paint next. This time use the colored part of the eye as a guide to paint the black. Try to leave an even amount of color all the way around the black.

4 After the paint has dried, add two to three coats of gloss varnish to the entire eye. It protects the paint from getting scratched off.

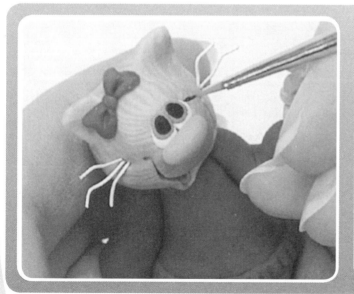

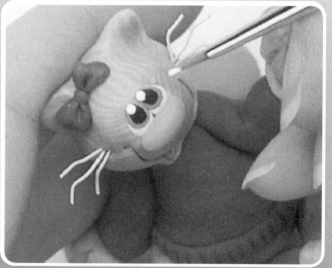

Arms and Hands

1 Make each arm from a $^7/_{16}$" flesh-colored clay ball. Roll the ball into one $^1/_4$" long log.

2 Flatten $^1/_4$" of the bottom of the log. This will become the hand.

3 Make the fingers and thumbs from $^1/_8$" flesh-colored balls of clay formed into $^1/_4$" long teardrops.

4 Place four teardrops on the palm of the hand so the rounded ends are visible from the other side. Place the thumb on the side of the hand.

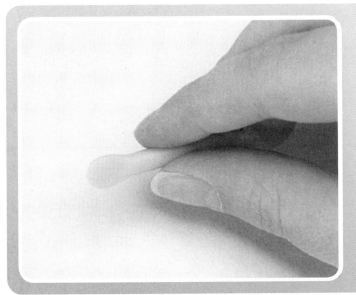 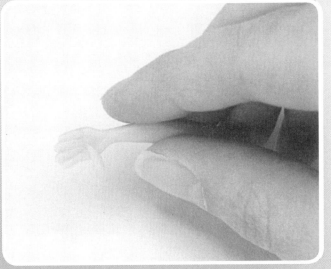

Tips & Quips: The sizes for the arms and hands shown here and for legs and feet (below) are standard for all projects.

5 Use the blending tool to blend the points of the teardrops into the palm of the hand.

6 The top side of a hand should look as it does in the photo.

7 The needle tool can be used to make an impression on the palm where the hand would naturally crease.

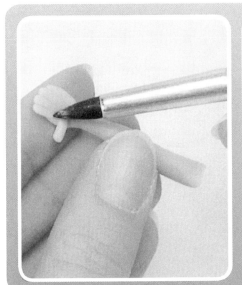 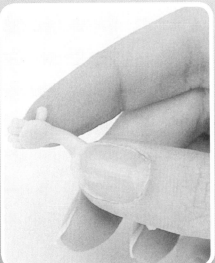 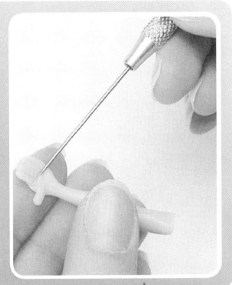

Continues

Legs and Feet

1 Make each leg from a $\frac{1}{4}$" flesh-colored ball rolled into one $\frac{3}{4}$" log.

2 Bend the end of the log upward to create the foot.

3 Roll what should be the ankle gently between your finger and thumb. Use your fingers to gently pinch the heel a tiny bit.

4 With the bottom of the foot facing you, pinch the bottom part of the heel so that the foot tapers at the bottom.

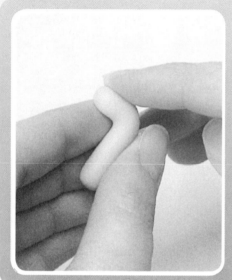
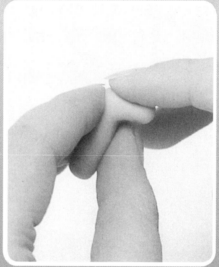
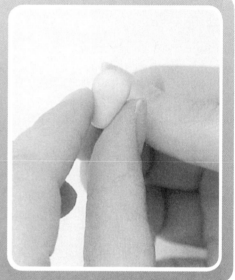

5 Use the side of your finger to make an arch in the foot.

6 Pinch the top of the foot a tiny bit. Whatever foot you just made, you'll need to repeat the process to make a right or left one.

7 Add the toes last. Make each big toe from a $\frac{3}{16}$" flesh-colored ball and each small toe from a $\frac{1}{8}$" flesh-colored ball. Put the big toe on first, then the four smaller ones.

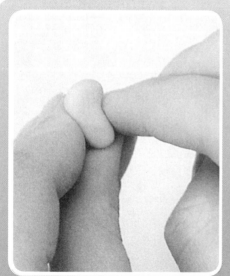
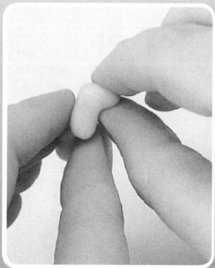

Skinner Blend

Many unique things can be created with a Skinner Blend, from making beautiful cane components to wonderful backgrounds. This technique was developed and published by Judith Skinner, hence the name Skinner Blend. A Skinner Blend can be made with a number of different colors, but in this example two are used.

1 Begin with two triangles of color. Place them together using the picture as a guide.

2 Following the diagram, fold the slabs of clay in half.

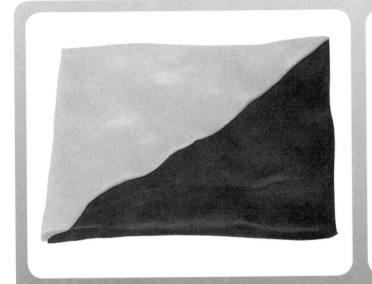

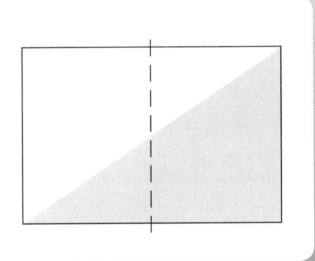

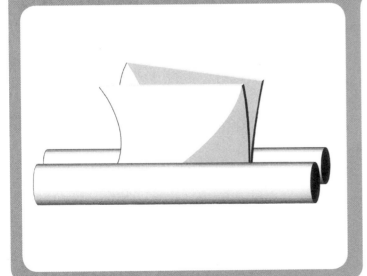

3 Place the clay in the pasta machine (or use a roller and wooden strips) with the fold going into the rollers first. The end corners will meet to form a square. Here, the back half of the rectangle in the diagram is angled so that you can see how the ends meet color-wise. Repeat this process about twenty-five times to get a smooth blend. It is important that you put the clay in the pasta machine in the same direction each time.

Kneading Clay
Using a Pasta Machine

Throughout the book you'll find that having a pasta machine handy will save you time and energy. This doesn't mean that you have to have one to make projects in this book. When pasta machines were first mentioned in this section, there were alternatives for rolling and combining clay. Should you do decide to invest in a pasta machine, here is how to handle the clay using one.

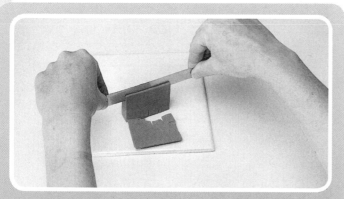

1 Unwrap a block of clay and stand it on its side. Use a blade to cut thin slices from the block. The slices should be about the same thickness as the thickest setting on your pasta machine to avoid straining the machine.

2 Roll each slice through the pasta machine. It will flatten into a sheet. Press the sheets together in pairs. Roll again, continuing until you have one large sheet. Fold the sheet in half and pass through again. Repeat this about 6 to 10 times, depending on soft the clay is.

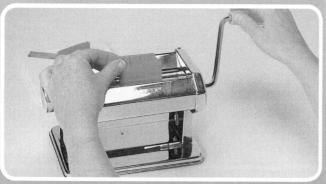

3 When you have folded a sheet of clay, make sure that you place the fold to the side as you pass it through the machine. This will help avoid trapping air in the clay. If you do get air bubbles, fold them to the outside and they will disappear with repeated rollings.

Creating Logs and Balls

This is a basic skill you should learn so that you can freely experiment at your leisure. Understanding the steps that follow will help when you are ready to tackle more complicated projects, as these steps are the foundation for most.

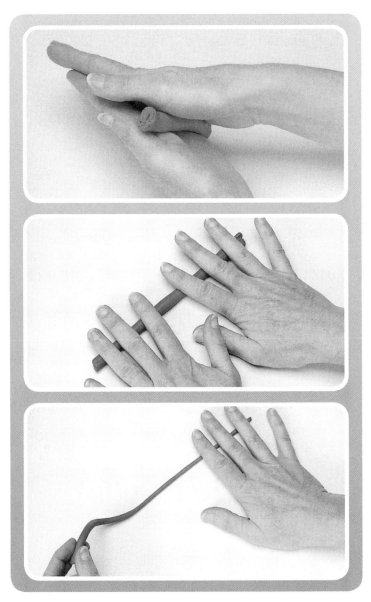

1 Squeeze the kneaded clay roughly into a log shape in your hands. Roll it back and forth between your palms. The log will smoothen and lengthen.

2 Lay the log on your work surface. Roll it back and forth with your fingers spread out lightly on the clay. Keep your fingers moving constantly from side to side along the length of the log to prevent the clay from becoming too thin in spots. Roll lightly or you will squash some areas and the log will not be even. With practice, you will be able to master this skill and create long, even logs of clay.

3 Some projects will require very thin logs. To create logs of $^1/_{16}$" thickness, first create a $^1/_4$" log. Hold one end in one hand and use the other to roll out the other end, thinning it as you roll. Keep your hand moving back and forth as before. The thicker part will provide a handle for controlling the thinner part so you do not have to touch the thin thread of clay once it has been formed.

Continues

4 To form a ball, place a piece of clay between your palms and, holding the lower hand still, apply light pressure with your upper hand, rotating it in small circles. Open your hands to see how round the ball has become and continue as necessary until you find the right amount of pressure to form a perfect little ball.

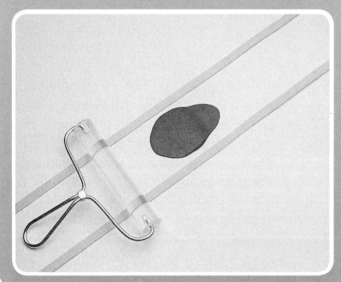

Tips & Quips: Wondering what the heck you're supposed to do with wooden strips when you're using a roller? Use the strips to place on either side of the clay to test the thickness of the clay. When you roll over the clay, you should be able to tell if some of the clay is thicker or thinner than other parts.

Marbling

This is easily done and will not work well if you use your pasta machine.

Follow the steps below to get the best possible marbling results.

1 Roll the colors you want marbled into equal-length logs. Depending on the proportions, the logs may not be the same thickness.

2 Press the two logs together and roll them in your hands until they have doubled in length.

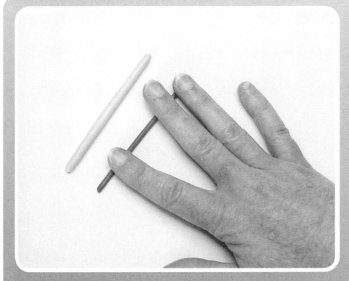

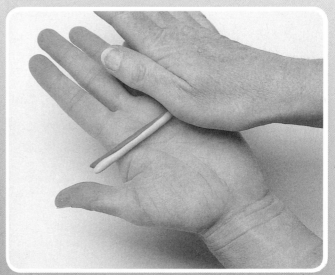

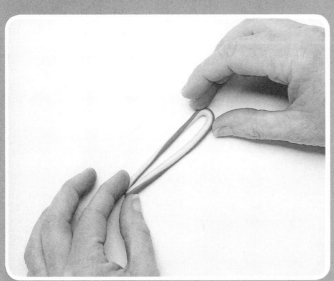

3 Fold the log in half. Be careful not to twist it. You want the two colors visible in straight lines all along the length.

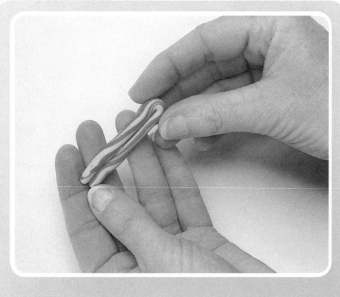

4 Roll and fold again in the same manner; continue until the lines are thin stripes. If you are going to roll the log into a marbled sheet, continue rolling and folding until the lines are very thin because they will spread once they are rolled flat.

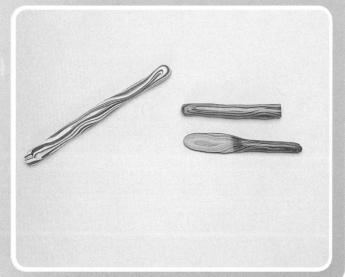

5 Here are the finished marbled pieces. Strong, contrasting colors work best.

Part II

Home Sweet Home

Starry Clock

Create this clock to dress up a spare bedroom or put it by the doorway so you will never be late. Inspired by an Arabian palace, this project makes a great gift, too.

Must-Haves: Materials

Tracing paper and thin cardstock • 2-ounce blocks of PREMO! Sculpey polymer clay: 2 pearl, $^1/_8$ block of gold, $^1/_{16}$ block of ultramarine blue, small amounts of burnt umber and alizarin crimson • Several ceramic tiles • Pasta machine (or use a roller and wood strips) • Talcum powder • Cutters (the ones that were used for this project are listed below)

- $^3/_8$" triangle cutter
- $^3/_8$" star cutter
- $^3/_{16}$" flower cutter
- $^3/_{16}$" heart cutter

• Craft knife • Needle • Pin • A brush protector or circle cutter about $^3/_8$" in diameter, or wide enough to cut a hole for the clock spindle to pass through • PVA glue • Quartz clockworks and filigree-style hands

1 Trace the clock front outline from the template below onto thin cardstock and cut it out.

2 Trace and cut out, separately, the two circles of the clock face to use later. Roll out a block of pearl clay until it is evenly shiny and $\frac{1}{16}$" thick. Lay this on a large tile and cut out the clock front using the template.

Mix It Up!

Marble the following:

Light blue marble = $\frac{1}{2}$ block of pearl + $\frac{1}{16}$ block ultramarine

Light gold marble = $\frac{1}{4}$ block of pearl + $\frac{1}{8}$ block gold

Old rose marble = $\frac{1}{4}$ block of pearl + a pea size each of the alizarin crimson and burnt umber

3 Roll out the marbled light gold clay on another tile at one setting thinner on your pasta machine. (If you are rolling by hand, roll the clay a little thinner with your roller.)

4 Sprinkle a dusting of talcum powder on the surface to prevent sticking, and use the triangle cutter to cut out lots of small triangles.

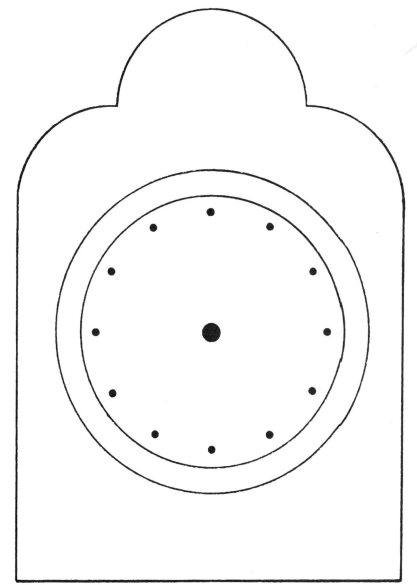

Clock Template

Cut Triangles

Continues →

5 Use your knife to lift each triangle into place on the front of the clock, working round the arches, and laying the edge of each triangle along the border of the clock. To turn the corner between two arches, cut a triangle in half and angle the two halves outward. See the photo at right.

Add Triangles

6 To make the inlaid stars, brush the clock surface with talc and use the star cutter to cut out three stars in the center of the middle arch. Remove the clay using the point of a needle, taking care not to damage the clock front.

Cut Out Stars

7 Roll out the light blue marble clay to the same thickness as the light gold clay. Cut out stars in the same way as for the triangles and carefully insert them into the star spaces on the clock's front.

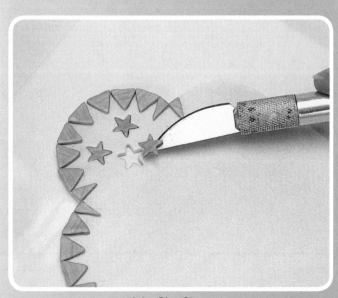

Inlay Blue Stars

Cut Out Flowers

8 The side arches each have an inlaid star flanked by two tiny flowers. Cut out and insert the inlaid stars in the same way as before, but use marbled light gold clay. Now use the tiny flower cutter to cut out the small flower shapes, one inside each star and one on either side of the star.

Repeat Inlay

9 Roll out the marbled old rose clay at the same thickness as the light gold clay. Cut and insert the tiny flower shapes as before. Use your knife tip to place the tiny pieces in position. Press over the inlays lightly with your fingertip to secure them in place.

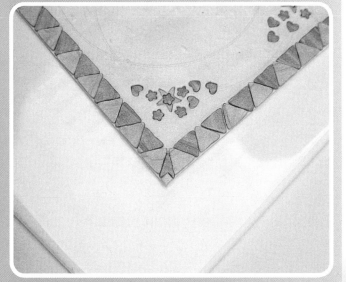

Finish Clock Face Additions

10 Work around the rest of the clock front, using the photos as a guide for positioning the inlays and applied triangles. The bottom part of the clock has light blue triangles alternating with light gold, and you will need to cut down the triangles to make neat corners. Use a combination of stars, hearts, and flowers to decorate each bottom corner.

Continues

11 Lay the large circle template on the clock front and push a pin through the center of the card to mark the point where the clock works spindle should go.

12 Use a brush protector or circle cutter to cut out a hole, centered on this exact spot and just wide enough for the spindle to pass through.

Mark Clock's Center

13 Roll out a sheet of pearl clay on a tile, at a thinner setting than the main clock front, and use the small circle template to cut out a circle for the block face.

14 Mark the center with a pin as before and cut out the hole for the spindle exactly in the center. Prick holes to mark the positions for the motifs that will be used instead of the clock numbers.

Create Pearl Clay Clock Face

15 Use the star cutter to inlay the top, bottom, and side stars of the clock face with light gold clay.

16 Use the flower cutter to inlay the light blue flowers that mark the remaining points of the clock face.

17 Use the star cutter to impress stars onto the central area of the face in a regular pattern.

18 Cut a $^{1}/_{16}$" thick strip of light gold from the gold sheet and wrap this around the outside of the face, butting and smoothing the joined clay.

Decorate

Attach Face to Clock

19 Use the larger circle template to cut out the clock face backing in light blue clay, and make a hole in the center for the spindle as before.

20 Bake all the pieces on their tiles for thirty to forty minutes. Keep checking the pearl clay as it can brown if your oven gets too hot. Allow the pieces to cool and remove from the tiles.

21 Use PVA glue to adhere the blue circle to the clock front, matching the spindle holes. Then glue the clock face on top of the blue circle, again matching the holes exactly.

Assemble Clock

22 Insert the hanger provided onto the clockworks before you assemble the clock. Push the spindle of the clock works through the spindle hole in the clock. Screw on the spindle screw until the clock works are held firmly on the back of the clock with the hanger at the top.

23 Push on the hour hand and then the minute hand. Adjust their positions to a whole hour. Screw down the smaller spindle screw to hold the hands in place.

Remember: The clock can be hung on the wall by the metal hanger at the back of the clockworks. Clockworks can vary in design, so if yours is slightly different, follow the instructions provided.

Adjust Clock Hands

Vintage Frame

Picture frames can be costly, especially the gilded variety. With a few simple tools and a bit of clay, you can quickly create a lovely frame to show off a treasured photo.

Must-Haves: Materials

Polymer clay: 1 black block, 2 gold blocks • Pasta machine (or use a roller and wooden strips) • Tile • Gold pearlized powder • Flat paintbrush • Field of flowers rubber stamp • Black pigment rubber stamp pad • Craft knife • 2¾" heart cookie cutter • Gold leaf foil • Superglue • 2 sheets 8½" × 11" lightweight cardboard • Ruler • Ball-tip stylus • Double-sided adhesive • Matte acrylic spray

Create Finish

1 Roll one block of gold clay through the largest setting of the pasta machine (or use a roller and wooden strips). Lay the clay sheet on a ceramic tile. Using the dry paintbrush, cover the surface of the clay with gold pearlized powder.

Stamp Gold Clay

2 Ink the rubber stamp and impress the clay. Apply enough pressure to leave a deep impression. Your finished frame will measure 4" × 5", so be sure your stamp covers a large surface.

Trim Stamped Clay

3 With a clay blade, trim the clay to 4" × 5". Cut out an opening from the center of the clay with a 2¾"-wide heart-shaped cookie cutter and remove the excess clay.

Continues

31

4 Roll ¼ block of black clay into a 5" log. Wrap the log in a sheet of gold leaf.

5 Cut away any excess leaf foil. Roll the foiled clay into a 20" log, ³/₈" in diameter.

Create Foiled Border

6 Superglue the log around the outside edges of the stamped clay. Press the foiled log firmly against the glued edges to secure. Trim any excess clay.

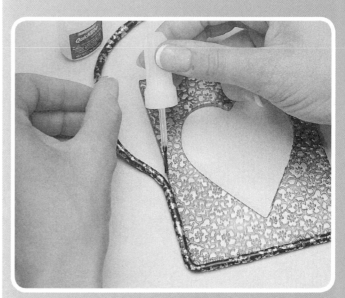
Glue Outside Border

7 Roll the remaining foiled clay log into a 10" log ¹/₈" in diameter. Superglue this log to the inside edge of the heart opening.

8 Cut off the excess clay and bake the frame on a tile at 270°F for thirty minutes. Then allow the frame to cool.

Add Inside Border

9 Cut out the cardboard backing of the frame with a craft knife, following the purple lines of the templates below.

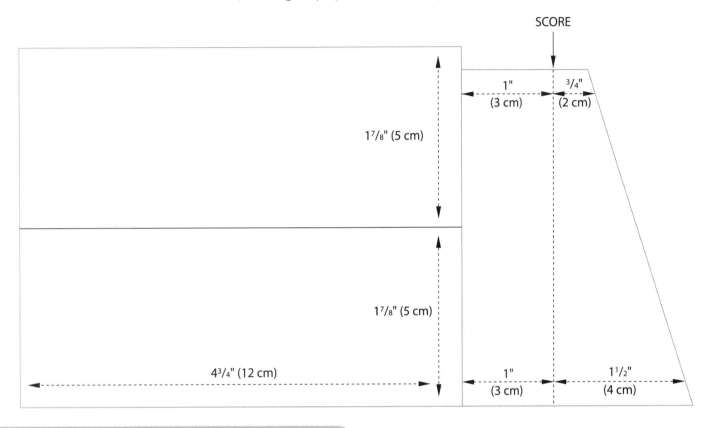

SCORE

1" (3 cm)

³/₄" (2 cm)

1⁷/₈" (5 cm)

1⁷/₈" (5 cm)

4³/₄" (12 cm)

1" (3 cm)

1¹/₂" (4 cm)

Create Easel Backing

10 On the easel backing, score from the top to the bottom points of the score line with a ruler and a ball-tip stylus. Fold at the score line.

11 Apply double-sided adhesive, aligning the bottom of the glued section with the center and the bottom of the frame backing.

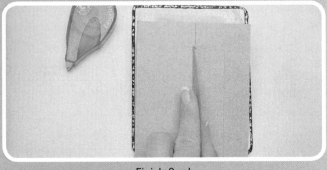

Finish Card

12 Lightly spray the cooled clay with matte acrylic spray. When dry, center your chosen photo behind the heart-shaped opening of the cooled frame. Apply double-sided adhesive to the backing and attach it to the frame.

Haunted Candle Lamp

This little house is great fun to make! Feel free to create your own template to make a unique haunted house for Halloween!

Must-Haves: Materials

Tracing paper and pencil • Scissors • 2-ounce block of black polymer clay • Three ceramic tiles at least 6" square • Craft knife • Roller • Brush protector or ¼" round cutter • Blunt tapestry needle • Transparent Liquid Sculpey • Oil paint: red, yellow, green, blue • Superglue • Votive candle and small jar to hold it

House Templates

1 Trace the three house pieces from the template and cut them out.

2 Roll out a sheet of black clay, about $1/16$" thick, and place on a tile. Lay the tracing for the house front on the sheet and cut it out.

Cut out Windows

3 Cut out the window shapes neatly with the point of your knife and pull out the extra clay.

Cut Scalloped Edge

4 Use the brush protector to cut a scalloped edge along the bottom edges of the roof. Hold the brush protector at an angle and make scalloped impressions across the front of the house to continue the bottom line of the roof.

Continues

5 Mark the edge of the door using the tapestry needle and make a hole in the top center of the door to suggest a small, round, decorative window.

Detail the Door

6 Form a ¼" thick log of black clay and roll one end into a thin length about $^1/_{16}$" thick and 2" long.

7 Hold the log by the thick end so that you have control and lay the thin end down the center of one of the windows. Trim it to length and press the two ends against the top and bottom of the window frame to secure them. Repeat to make a line across the window. Divide the other windows into panes in the same way.

Detail the Windows

8 Cut out the house sides from black clay sheets on two more tiles and cut scallops along each roof side with the brush protector.

9 Cut out the rose window on the left house side using the brush protector. First cut out the central round pane to position the window, then cut the surrounding panes.

Make House Sides

10 Form a $^1/_{16}$" thick log of black clay and cut four $^3/_8$" lengths for the cat's legs. Press these down on the tile in two pairs with a slight gap between the pairs.

11 Form a $^3/_8$" ball of black clay and shape it into an oval. Flatten it a little and press down over the tops of the legs, angling the left side upward to suggest an arching back.

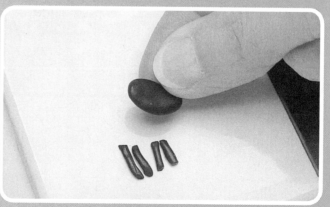

Create the Cat

Add Head and Tail

12 Flatten a $\frac{1}{4}$" ball of black clay and press onto the right side for the head.

13 Form a $\frac{1}{16}$" thick log, $\frac{3}{4}$" long, and point one end for the tail. Press onto the cat's rear, curving it over its back.

Detail the Cat

14 Form two tiny cones of black clay and press onto the top of the head for the ears.

15 Mark eyes and mouth with the tip of your tapestry needle. If you make holes right through the clay, the cat's eyes will light up when the candle is lit!

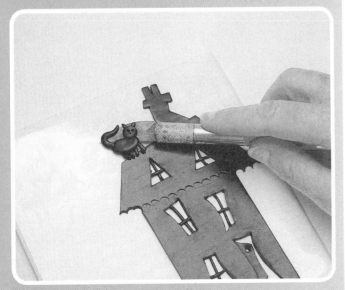

Add Cat to House

16 Slice under the cat with your knife to free it from the tile and position it on the roof of the house. Press it down firmly to attach it to the roof—the cat's feet should overlap the top of the roof for strength.

Continues

17 Pour some Transparent Liquid Sculpey onto a palette and use the tapestry needle to scoop it up and drip it into several of the window areas. Fill the windows fairly thickly, but do not allow the liquid to flow over the top of the logs dividing the panes.

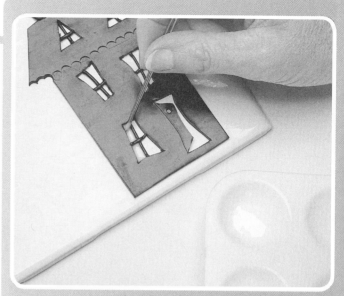

Apply Liquid Sculpey

18 For the colored windows, mix a tiny dab of oil paint into the Liquid Sculpey to make a pastel color. Use it for the white windows. If you drip any Liquid Sculpey onto the surface of the house, wipe it away gently with a tissue.

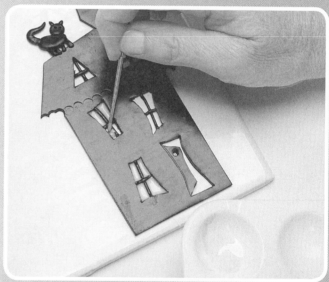

Color in Windows

19 Bake all three house pieces on their tiles for forty-five minutes and allow to cool. The pieces need to be strong, so make sure the clay has baked all the way through.

20 Carefully remove the pieces from the tiles. The windows will have set into a flexible, translucent layer.

21 Use superglue to adhere the two sides of the house at right angles to the house front. The house will stand up securely on three sides. Place a candle or votive in a small glass jar inside the house and enjoy!

Note: Take care that the candle flame does not come into contact with the polymer clay walls of the house or they will burn. It is safest to place the candle inside a small candleholder or jelly or baby food jar.

Assemble the House

Stamp-a-Votive

A perfect gift for friends, this project can be colored any way you wish or even left sheer for a delicate look.

Must-Haves: Materials

Glass votive • White polymer clay • Pasta machine (or use a roller and wood strips) • Polymer clay blade • Cornstarch • Deeply etched stamp • Pink and gold PearlEx powder • Soft application brush • Damp cloth

1 Condition and prepare a thin layer of clay that will extend the circumference and height of the votive. (Use a middle setting on a pasta machine to achieve a $3/32$" thickness.)

2 Cover the glass with the clay, stretching it slightly where the glass bulges. Release any air bubbles and smooth the clay to the glass. The clay will adhere to the slick surface of the glass.

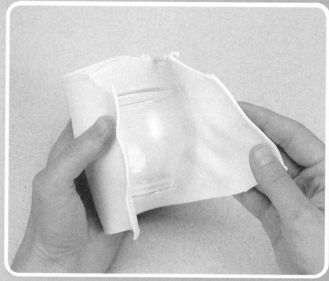

Cover Glass with Clay

3 Score the clay with the blade from top to bottom (vertically) to make a straight edge.

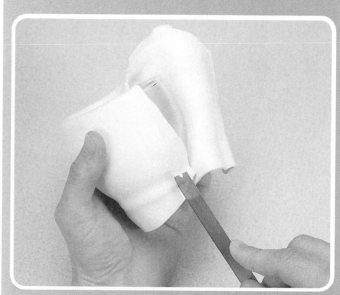

Score Clay

4 Overlap the clay just enough to indicate where the clay joins and slice vertically to remove any excess.

Remove Excess Clay

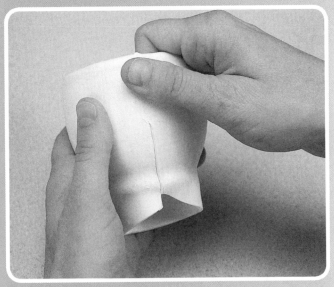

Smooth Seam

5 Smooth the seam with your fingers. You may need to dust your hands with cornstarch to help handle the clay so as to avoid leaving fingerprints in it.

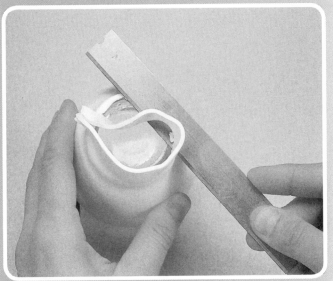

Trim Bottom

6 Trim the bottom of the votive with the blade and tuck the top edge inside the votive. (It will be trimmed after it is imprinted.)

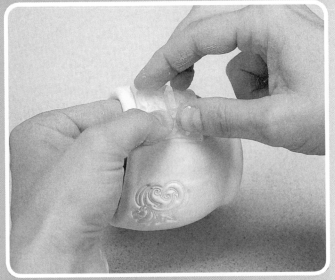

Stamp Clay

7 Dust the votive with a thin layer of cornstarch. Position a stamp to make a border around the top edge and press firmly. Stamp the next impression directly opposite the first. Slight overlapping or variations are fine. Be creative!

8 With your blade, trim the clay from the inside of the top using the glass edge as your guide.

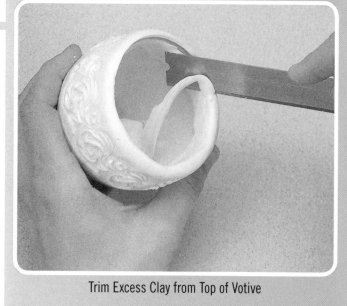

Trim Excess Clay from Top of Votive

9 Dust the clay with pink PearlEx. If the powder won't take due to excessive cornstarch, you can wipe the clay gently with a damp cloth.

Apply Pink PearlEx

10 Overlay a layer of gold PearlEx powder to create a blown-glass finish. The powder will work into the polymer clay. Some powder may rub off after baking, but it will have a pearlescent shimmer. Bake as the manufacturer's instructions indicate.

Tips & Quips: Brush up! Try using a brush (an old makeup brush works fine) to allow the PearlEx to seep into the crevices.

Overlay a Layer of Gold PearlEx

Cool Cutlery

Why not dress up some utensils with fabulous whorls of almost holographic patterns? The classy (and hand-washable) look is created using millefiori caning techniques with pearlescent PREMO! Sculpey. This remarkable technique was first developed by Pier Voulkos, Mike Buesseler and others in the United States. The effects do not work with other pearl or metallic polymer clays so you will need to use pearlescent clay that contains mica particles such as PREMO! Sculpey.

Must-Haves: Materials

2-ounce blocks of PREMO! Sculpey polymer clay: 2 pearl, 1 blue pearl • Pasta machine (or use a roller and wood strips) • Sharp blade • Tile (optional) • Stainless steel cutlery in a simple design • Pin

1 Roll out a sheet of light blue pearl clay, fold in half and roll again. Repeat several times until the surface of the clay is uniformly shiny.

2 Roll out the sheet about $^1/_8$" thick and lay it on a tile or hard surface. Trim the edges to make a rectangle 4" × 6".

Make Rectangle

Mix It Up!

Mix together the following:

Light blue pearl = 2 parts pearl + 1 part blue pearl

3 Cut the rectangle in half and place one half on top of the other. Cut in half again, and again stack the two halves one on top of the other. Repeat once more to make a stacked block approximately 1½" wide, 2" long, and 1" tall.

Cut Sheets

4 Trim the edges of the block. You will find that while the top surface of the block is shiny, when you take a slice from any of the sides, it has a dull appearance. This is normal.

Trim Edges of Block

Stack Shiny and Dull Sheets

5 Roll out another shiny sheet of light blue pearl, as thin as you can—about $1/32$" thick.

6 Cut a rectangle 2" wide and 5" long. Lay this on the tile. Now cut slices from the dull long side of your block, about $1/32$" thick. Lay these side by side on top of the shiny rectangular sheet.

7 Butt the edges of the slices together so that there are no gaps.

Press Joins and Trim

8 When the rectangle is covered with dull sheets, press the joins together lightly to consolidate them and trim the double sheet if necessary.

9 Press along the edge of one of the short ends to flatten it.

Roll Clay

10 Ease the flattened edge off the tile and, beginning at this end, roll up the two sheets together tightly like a jellyroll. As you roll, press gently to expel any air bubbles that might be caught inside the roll.

Continues

11 When the two sheets are tightly rolled up together, press lightly to consolidate the roll. You now have a cane for slicing, but do not try to reduce it or the effects will be lost.

12 Cut a slice off one end to trim it and then cut lots of $1/16$" thick slices. Keep your blade as vertical as possible and try to cut the slices evenly and of the same thickness. The spiral effect of rolling the two sheets together is already very clear.

Slice Cane

13 Roll out a sheet of shiny clay at the thickest setting on your pasta machine (or use a roller and wood strips), about $1/8$" thick. Position the slices of spiral cane in a regular pattern.

Create the Veneer

14 Pass the sheet with the applied slices through your pasta machine on the same thickest setting on the machine (or roll over the sheet lightly with your roller).

15 Apply another layer of slices, slightly overlapping the first slices.

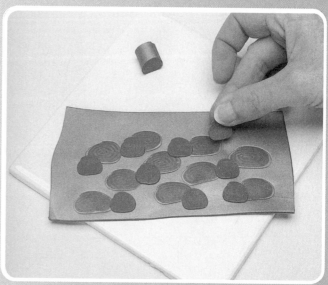

Apply More Slices

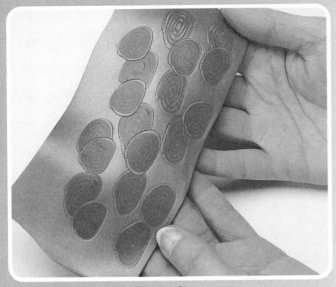

Thin the Sheet

16 Pass the sheet through the pasta machine again in the same direction as before, keeping the machine on the same setting.

17 Set the pasta machine to roll at about $^1/_{16}$" thick, a medium setting, and pass the sheet through again. This will smooth the surface and accentuate the effect.

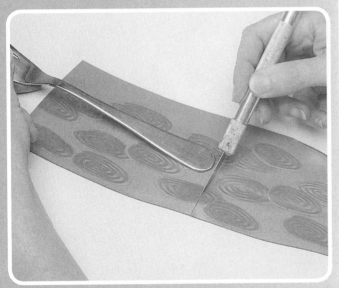

Cut Clay for Handle

18 Pass the sheet through one last time at one setting thinner. The spiral lozenges will elongate and look like flying saucers on a background of light blue. Lay the handle of the fork on the sheet and cut out enough clay to cover the handle.

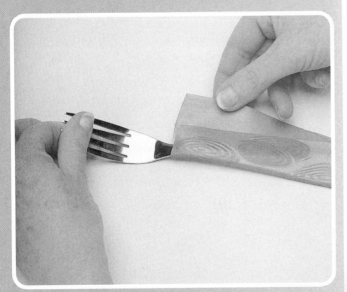

Cover Fork Handle

19 Turn the clay sheet over and lay the fork handle on the back. Fold the sheet over the top of the fork handle, moving it if necessary to position the patterning as desired.

20 Use a pair of scissors to trim the clay all along the fork handle, close to the edge, which you can feel through the clay.

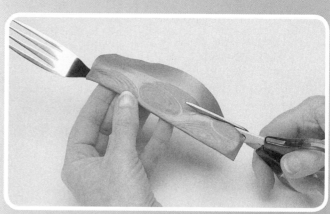

Trim Clay

21 Press the two edges of the sheet together along the side and end of the fork handle, smoothing the seam by using your fingers.

Join and Smooth Clay

22 Use a pin to pierce any bubbles that appear under the clay and press them to expel the air. If you do not do this, they will accentuate during baking as the air inside expands.

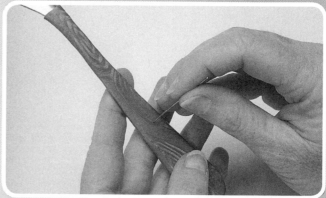

Remove Bubbles

23 Trim the top edge of the handle neatly. Repeat to cover the knife and spoon handles to make a matching set. Bake all the pieces on baking parchment for thirty minutes.

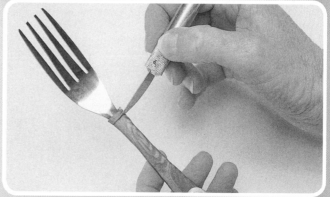

Trim Edges

Lovely Lampshade

Perfect for your living room or bedroom, use strong clay for this project such as PREMO! Sculpey, which is flexible when baked. Lampshade frames are available in all shapes and sizes. Choose a frame that has fairly straight sections so that you do not have to bend the baked clay sheets very much.

Must-Haves: Materials

Wire lampshade frame with the sides divided into 6 to 8 sections • Plain white sheet of paper, pencil, and scissors • 2-ounce blocks of polymer clay: 4 translucent, 1 golden yellow, 1 magenta, 1 red, 2 black (Note: These quantities are for a lampshade that measures 9$\frac{1}{2}$" tall and 14$\frac{1}{2}$" in diameter across the bottom. You may need to adjust the quantities depending on the size of your frame.) • Tile (optional) • Pasta machine (or use a roller and wooden strips) • Roller • Clay knife • Large cookie sheet lined with baking parchment • Superglue • Scrap clay for making the stamp • Charm or small piece of jewelry for the stamp • Talcum powder• Super Bronze PearlEx powder • Gloss varnish

1 Lay the lampshade on the paper and draw around the outside of one of the sections to make a panel template. Cut out the shape with scissors.

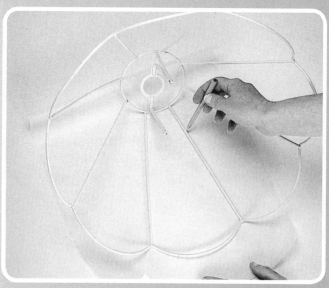

Make Template

2 Divide one of the blocks of translucent clay into three equal pieces. Each one of these pieces will be tinted a different color.

3 Take $^{1}/_{16}$ of a block of red clay and marble this into one of the translucent pieces to make longitudinal streaks (see page 21 for the Marbling technique). Repeat with the yellow and magenta clays.

Measure Clay

4 The marbled logs should look as they do in the photo below. The streaks are still visible and are ready to be turned into a marble sheet.

Form Marbled Logs

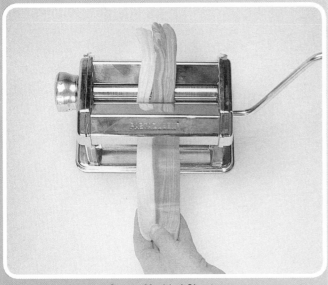

Create Marbled Sheets

5 Press the three logs together side by side with the red clay in the center. Flatten them in your hands and feed them through the widest setting on the pasta machine, end first, so that they form a sheet of clay with longitudinal streaks.

6 Pass the clay through the pasta machine again, in the same direction, at a medium setting of about $1/16$" thick.

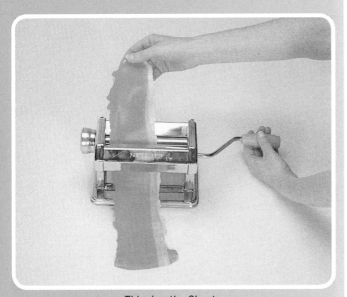

Thinning the Sheets

7 Fold the sheet in half and pass through the pasta machine again. This will begin to blend the clay and merge the colors where they have joined. Repeat several more times, folding and passing the clay through the machine longitudinally until you are satisfied with the results.

8 Roll the clay through on the thinnest setting that your pasta machine can handle without rumpling the clay. (If you are unsure of this, test with scrap clay first.)

Cutting out the Template

9 Cut the sheet in half across its middle with a clay knife and lay the two pieces side by side on a paper-covered surface so that the clay does not stick.

10 Flip one of the sheets so that the two magenta stripes are placed together. Overlap the joined stripes slightly and press all along them to seal the pieces into one sheet.

11 Center the paper template over the sheet and cut out the panel shape. Save all the scraps as you can marble them into the next sheet.

Continues

12 Repeat to make as many panels as your lampshade frame requires. Transfer the panels to a cookie sheet lined with baking parchment. Bake for thirty minutes to be sure that the clay is fully baked and strong.

13 Run a thin line of superglue around the edge of part of the frame. Press a clay panel on the glue, bending it to fit any curves and using scissors to trim the clay if necessary. Continue to do this around the frame, making sure that all the edges are glued down firmly.

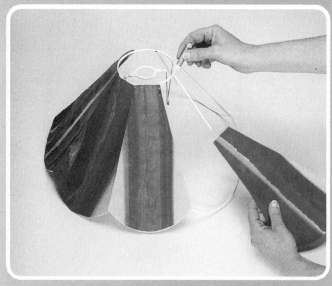

Attach Panels

14 Form a thick rope of black clay by twisting together two logs about $3/16$" thick to form a rope.

15 Lay the panel template on the cookie sheet and curve the rope around the base, trimming the ends to fit. Make as many curved ropes as your lampshade has panels.

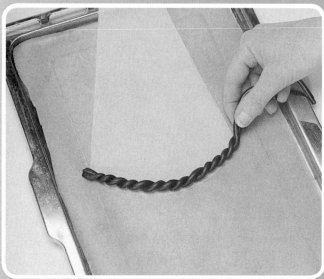

Make Trimmings

16 To make a stamp, knead a small ball of clay scraps. Flatten the ball onto a tile.

17 Brush the surface of the clay with talcum powder to prevent sticking, and press a small piece of jewelry firmly onto the clay surface.

18 Remove the jewelry and bake the stamp for twenty to thirty minutes.

Make Stamp

Create Medallions

19 Form some small balls of black clay. Shape each ball to match the shape of your stamp and press down onto the tile. Brush with talc and then impress each one with the stamp.

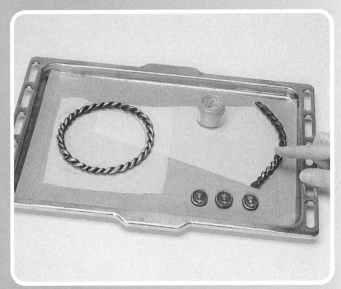

Make Top Ring

20 To make the top ring, turn the lampshade upside-down on a piece of paper and draw around the top to make a template.

21 Form a black rope of clay as you did in Step 14 and curve it around the template. Trim the ends and butt them together.

22 Dip your finger into the bronze powder and crush over the surface of all the black clay pieces. (Only the raised areas will be coated with bronze to give the appearance of rich antique metal.)

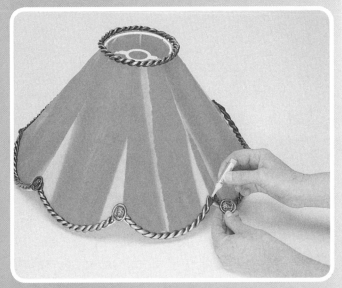

Attach Trimmings

23 Bake all the black pieces for thirty minutes. When cool, coat with gloss varnish to protect the powder.

24 Use superglue to stick the ropes around the bottom of the lampshade. Trim to fit, if necessary, with a craft knife.

25 Glue the top ring to the top of the lampshade. Glue the stamped medallions between each pair of curves, covering the cut ends.

Sentimental Circle

Use this cute container to store keepsakes, pictures, and any other loot close to your heart. Of course you can always make a smaller or larger box than the one pictured here.

Must-Haves: Materials

2-ounce pearl blocks of polymer clay • 12" metal ruler, about 1¼" wide • Paper towel insert, smoothly covered with foil and taped • Pasta machine (or use a roller and wood strips) • Craft knife • Tapestry needle • Darning needle • Ceramic tiles • Talcum powder • Fun-Tak or Blu-Tak (reusable putty adhesive) • Transparent Liquid Sculpey • Oil paint: white, blue, violet • Superglue • Sandpaper and quilt batting

Create Box Sides

1 Roll out the pearl clay into a sheet, fold in half and roll out again several times until uniformly shiny.

2 Roll the sheet to about $^3/_{32}$" thick. Lay the ruler on the sheet and use it as a cutting edge to cut a strip of clay $1^1/_4$" wide and about 8" long.

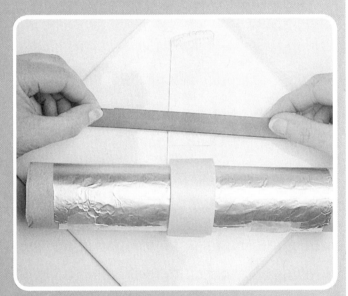

Roll Clay Around Former

3 Roll the clay strip around the foil-covered form, keeping the edges of the strip as straight as possible. Keep rolling until the beginning of the strip meets the clay surface again and makes a faint impression. Unroll a little and trim the clay on this line.

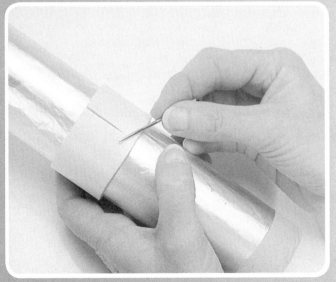

Join, Smooth, Bake

4 The strip should now be the right length for the two ends to meet. Smooth the seam with the side of a tapestry needle. Bake the box sides on the form for twenty minutes. Allow to cool and slip the baked clay off the former.

5 Roll out a $1/16$" thick sheet of pearl clay and lay it on the tile. Smear the clay surface with talc to prevent sticking and place the baked box sides on it.

6 Cut around the outside of the box for the lid, holding your knife blade as upright as possible for a neat edge. Remove the waste clay from around the lid and leave the lid on the tile.

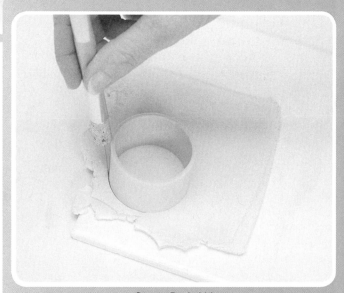

Create Box's Lid

7 Place the remaining sheet on a spare spot on the tile and press the box sides on again, firmly, to make an impression. Remove the box and cut around the inside of the resulting mark to make the inner lid. This will be glued to the underside of the lid after baking so that the lid fits snugly onto the box.

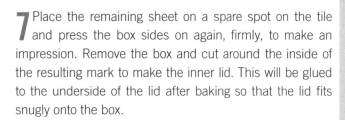

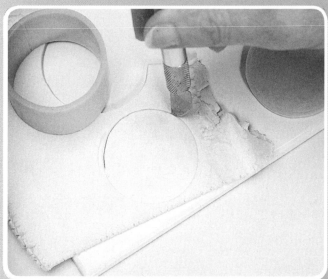

Make Lid Flange

8 Roll another $3/32$" thick sheet of pearl clay and, using no talcum powder this time, press the bottom of the box sides firmly onto the sheet. Cut around the outside and remove the waste clay.

9 Use your knife to smooth the seam between the soft clay of the box base and the base sides. Bake all the pieces on the tile for thirty minutes. When cool, sand and buff any rough areas.

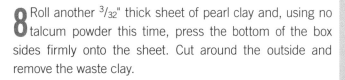

Make the Box's Base

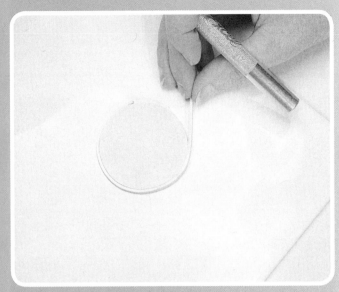

Refine Lid

10 Place the box on a tile, best side up. Cut an 8" long strip of clay, about $^1/_{16}$" wide, from a $^1/_{16}$" thick sheet. Wrap this around the outside of the lid, smoothing the joins. This will make the lid slightly larger in diameter than the box and will give a better finish.

Add Liquid Sculpey

11 Fix the lid to the tile with a tiny scrap of Fun-Tak underneath it to keep it from sliding around.

12 Brush a thin coat of Liquid Sculpey over the surface of the lid. Mix a little white oil paint into about a teaspoonful of Liquid Sculpey on your palette.

Tips & Quips: It is a good idea to practice the following steps on a tile or piece of scrap clay first.

13 Dip the tapestry needle tip into the white Liquid Sculpey to collect a drop on the end. Touch the center of the lid with the drop. Slowly lift the needle vertically up from the surface. A thread of Liquid Sculpey will extend from the needle and this will part and drop back as you lift, so keep the needle above the pool of color. Repeat to make four more pools around the central one. You will find that you can vary the size of the pool by altering the size of the drop on the end of the needle.

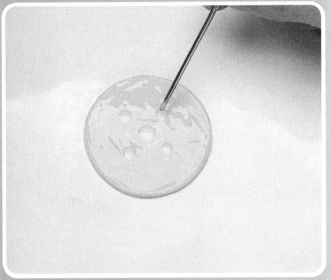

Create White Pools

14 Mix some blue oil paint into another teaspoon of Liquid Sculpey on your palette. Apply drops of this to the centers of each of the outer pools of white. Repeat with magenta for the centermost pool. Use the same technique of lifting the needle so that the thread of color parts vertically above the application point. If you take the needle sideways as you lift, the thread will make a trail to one side and spoil the effect. The drops of color should form perfect circles within the pools of white.

15 Apply another smaller drop of white in the center of each colored pool. To make the stars, draw the pointed tip of a darning needle from the center of each pool outward. Work around each star, pulling out eight points on each. It is easier to do this evenly by working in pairs—pull out the top and bottom points, then the two sides, and then the points in between.

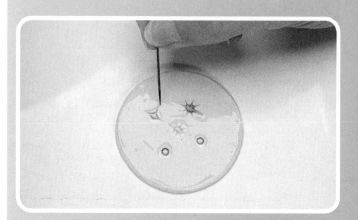

16 To make hearts, drop pools of white at regular intervals around the edge of the lid. Then drop in pools of violet. Draw the darning needle right through the center of each pool, starting on the side toward the center and ending at the edge of the lid. This will form a perfect heart.

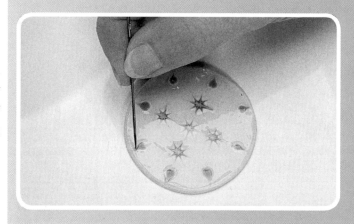

17 Bake the box lid on the tile for twenty minutes. When cool, attach the lid insert centrally to the underside of the lid with Fun-Tak. Push the lid onto the box to check the fit, adjust if necessary, and mark the position with a pencil. Glue in place with superglue.

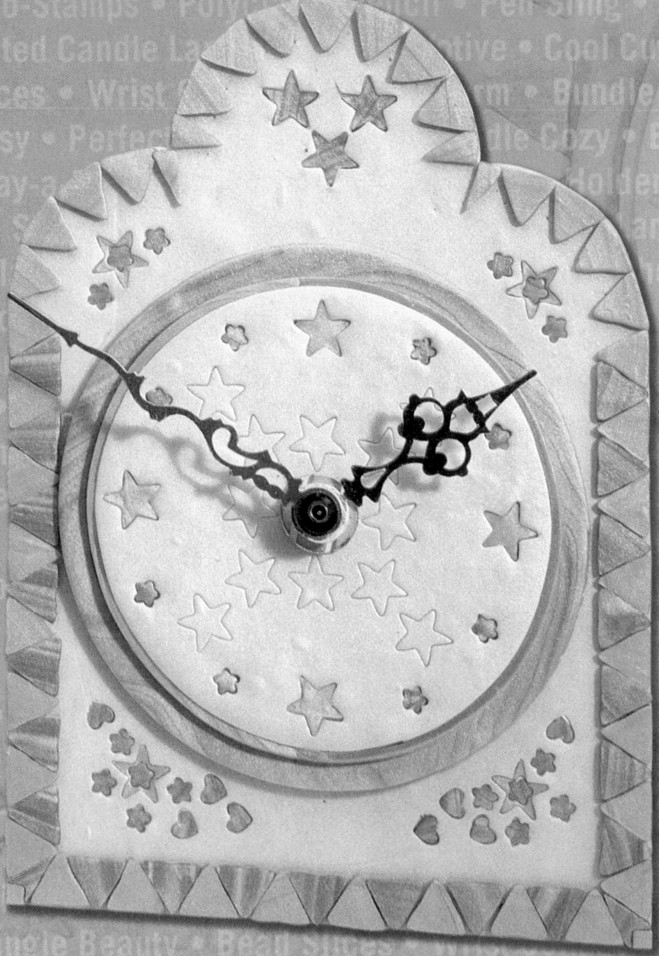

Starry Clock

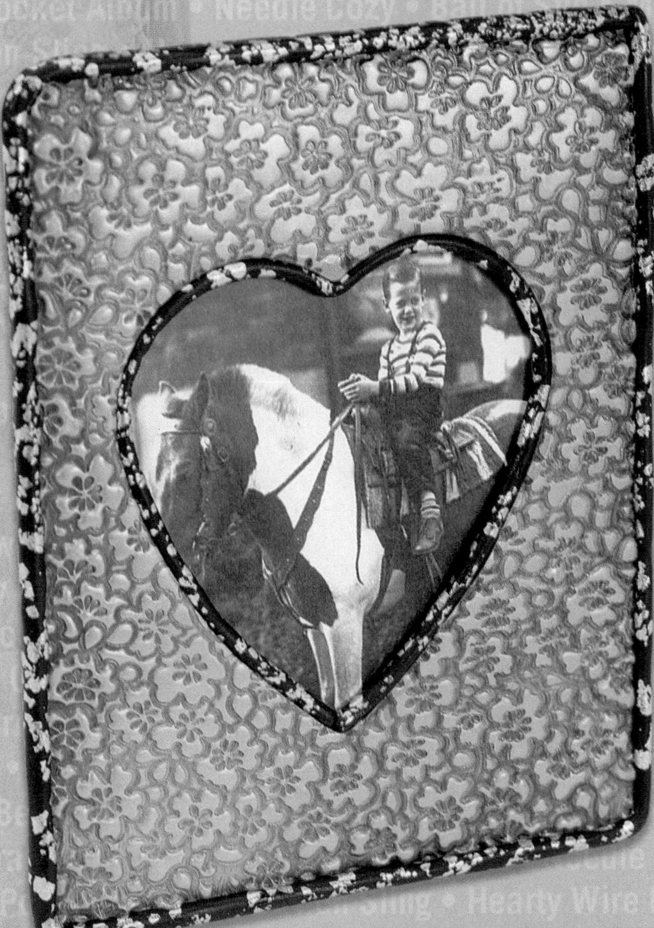

Vintage Frame

PAGE 34

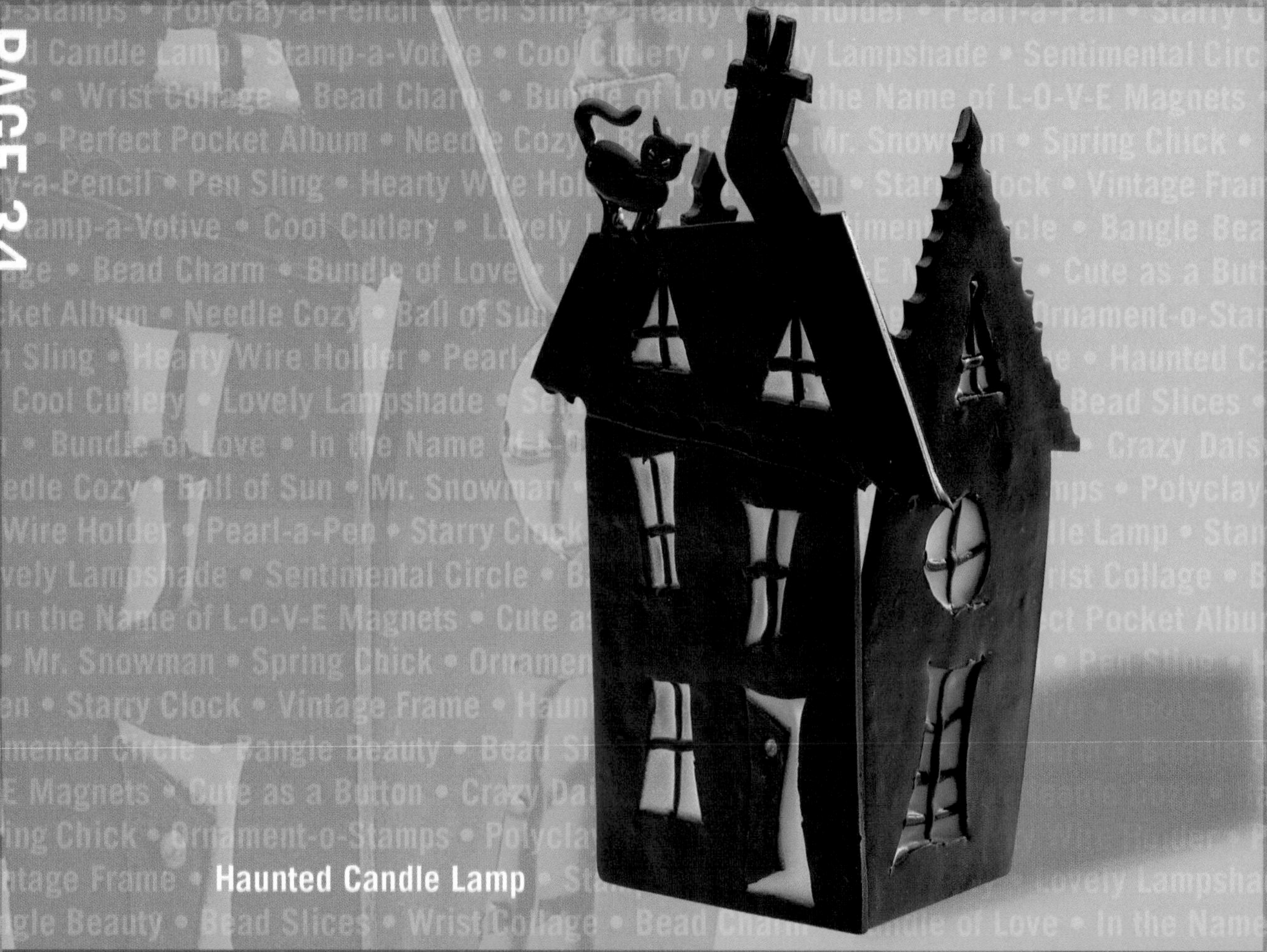

Haunted Candle Lamp

PAGE 39

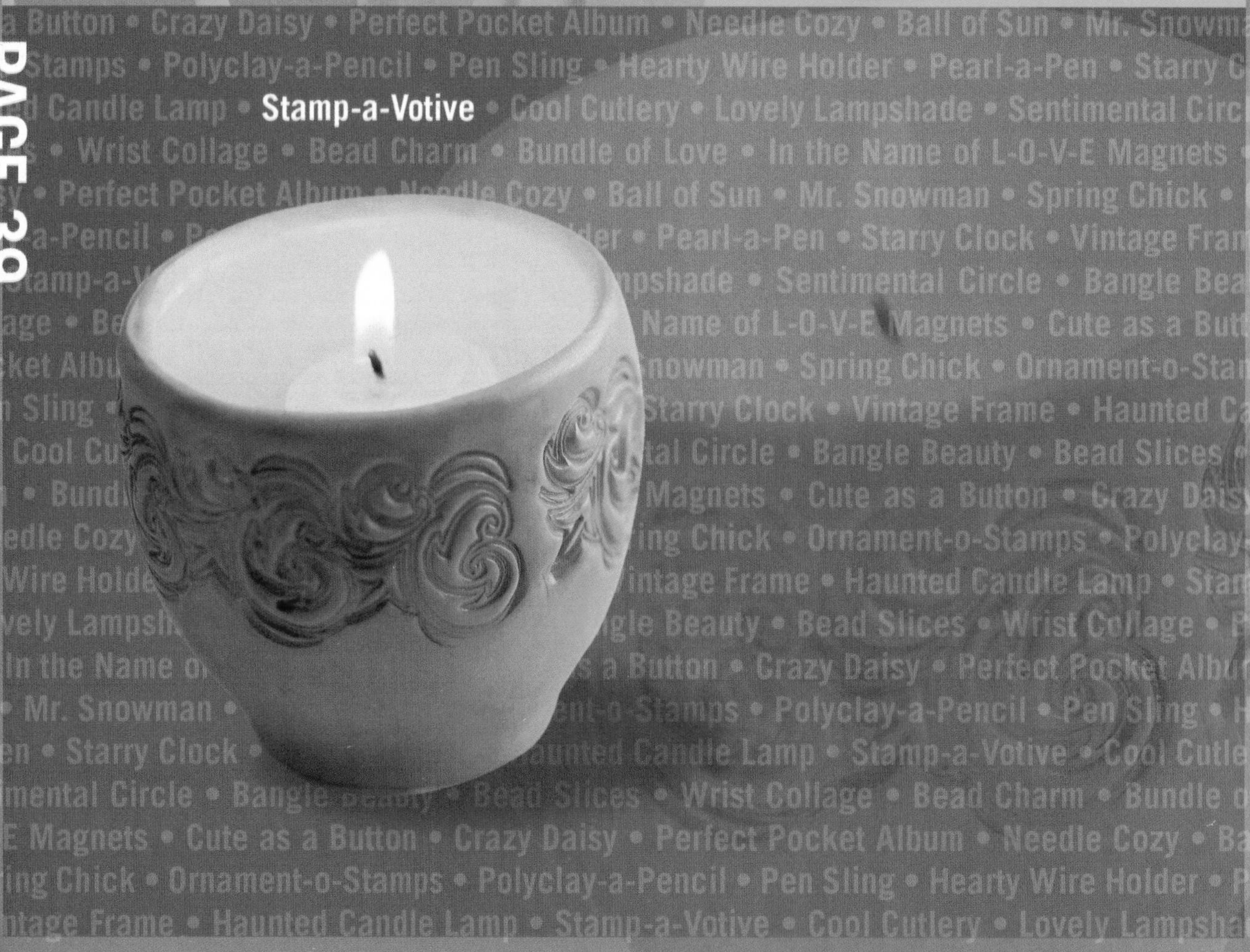

Stamp-a-Votive

Cool Cutlery

Lovely Lampshade

Bead Slices

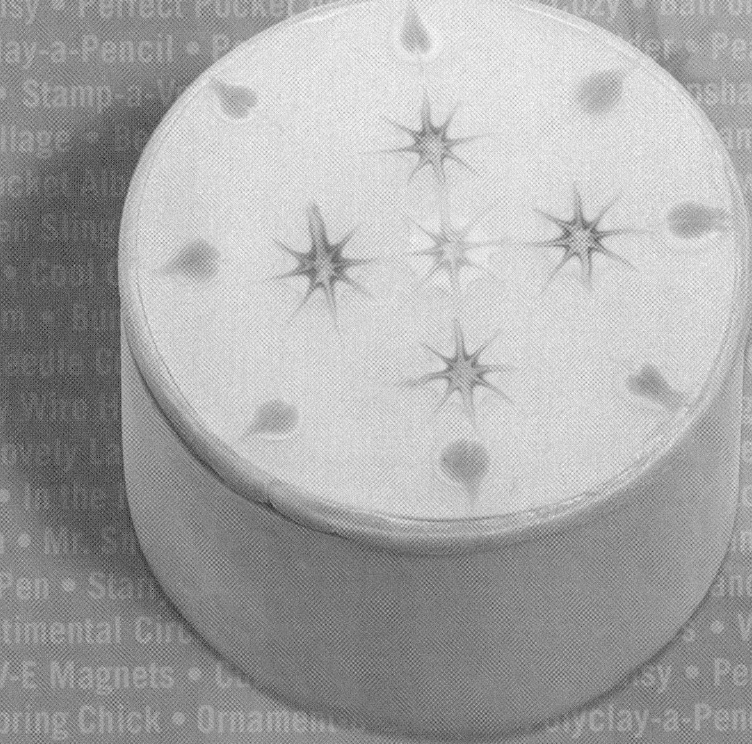

Sentimental Circle

PAGE 54

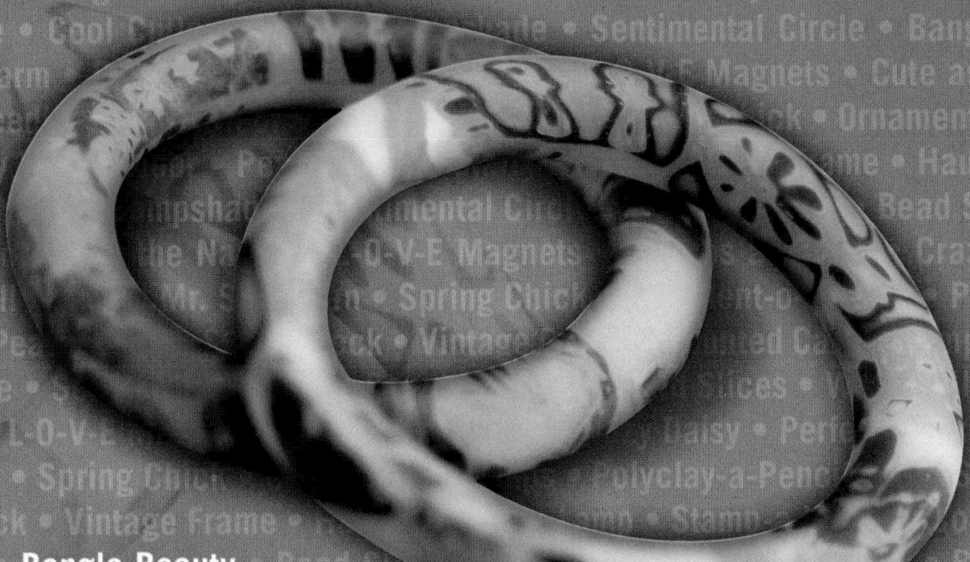

Bangle Beauty

PAGE 60

Wrist Collage

Bundle of Love

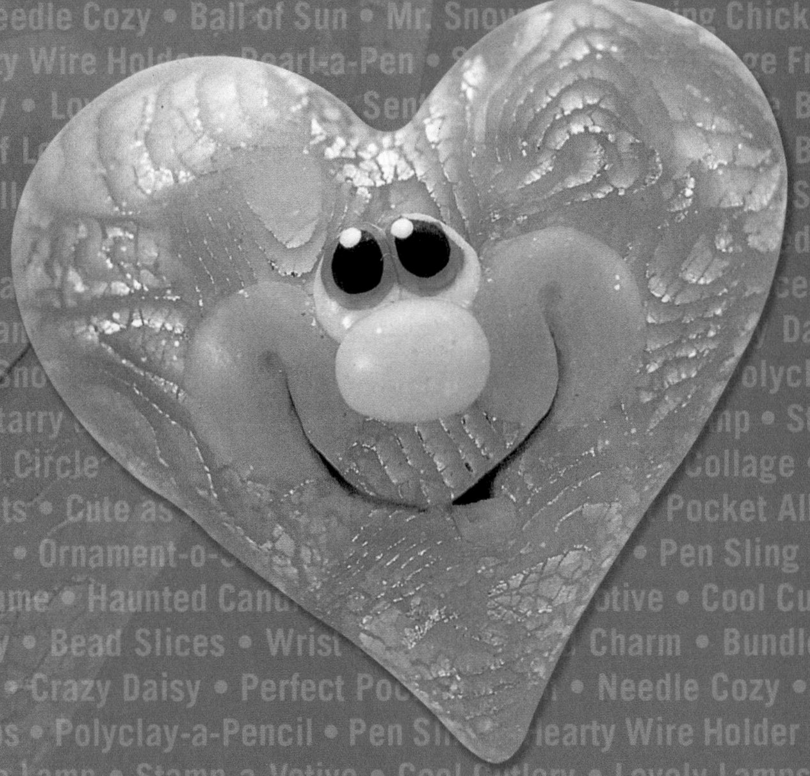

PAGE 77

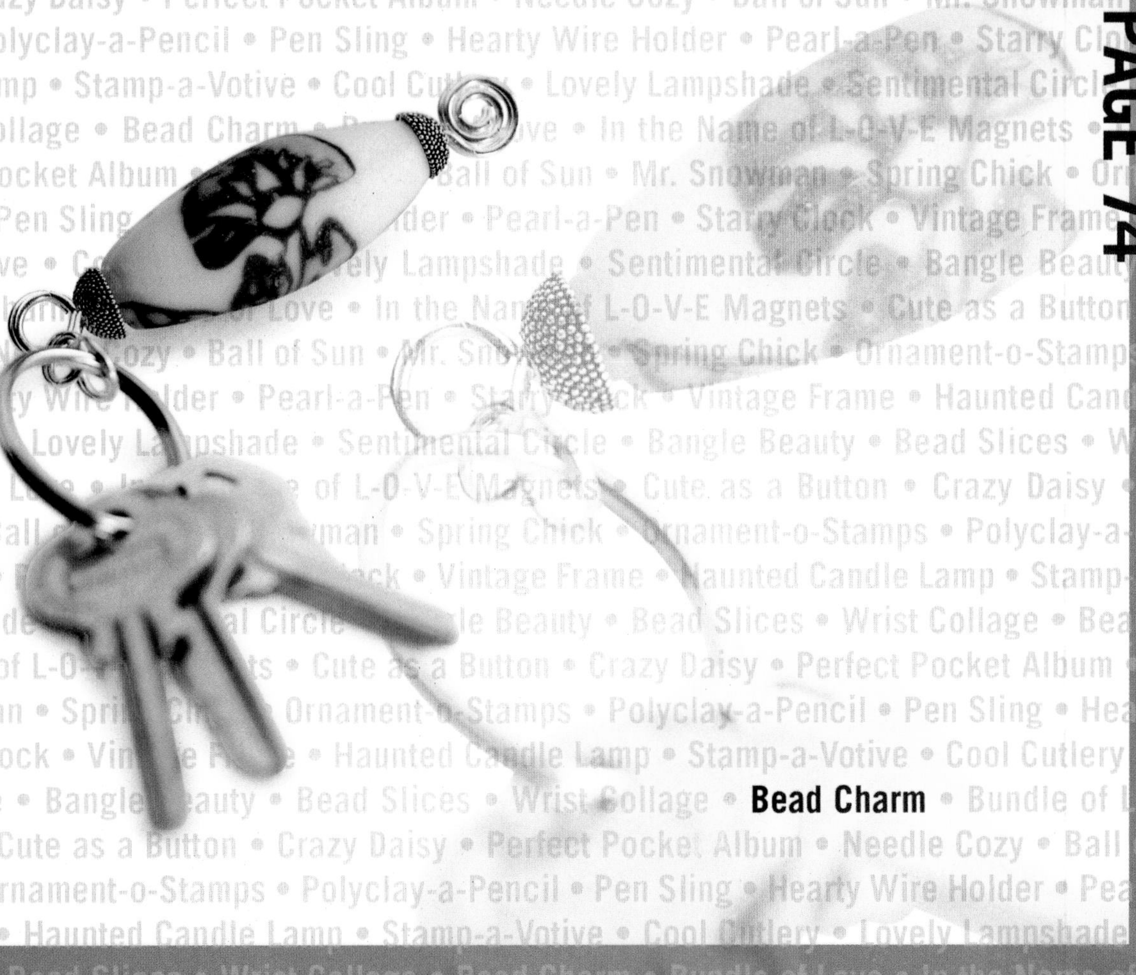

Bead Charm

PAGE 74

In the Name of L-O-V-E Magnets

Part III

Priceless Jewelry

Bangle Beauty
Bead Slices
Wrist Collage

Bangle Beauty

This dainty bracelet not only makes use of scrap clay, it also creates a veiled or subtle frosted look. The perfect accessory that goes with anything, why not make two matching ones: one for yourself and one for a best friend!

Must-Haves: Materials

Polymer clay: translucent, white • Scraps from another project • Gold PearlEx powder • Pasta machine (or use a roller and wooden strips) • Paper, tape, and scissors for measuring wrist • Polymer clay blade

Apply PearlEx and Press Scraps into Sheet

1 Condition and roll out a thin sheet of white clay about 2" to 8". This strip will become the outer decoration for the bracelet. Take the scraps from a previous project and place them on the white clay sheet.

2 Use your finger to apply a small amount of PearlEx powder, and press the scraps firmly into the sheet. Do not apply excessive amounts of powder.

Place Prepared Clay over Strip

3 Roll a long strip of translucent clay on the thinnest setting of the pasta machine (or use a roller and wooden strips). If the thinnest setting is not manageable, use a thicker setting and stretch the clay. Place it over the prepared strip.

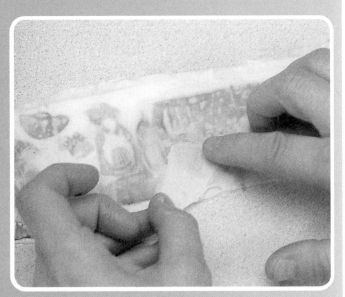

Press Clay Together

4 Press the clay together securely—you can make small patches with translucent clay if necessary. The goal is to have a very thin layer of translucent clay over your prepared strip.

Continues ➤

5 Roll a log of white clay about 8" long and ³/₈" wide. You can also use scrap clay, as it will be hidden inside the bracelet.

6 Cover the log with the prepared strip (this will increase the diameter).

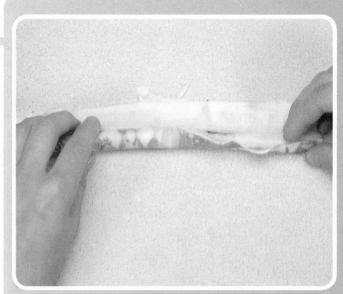
Roll Log of White Clay

7 Roll the band on a hard surface to smooth the seams and remove any debris from the surface.

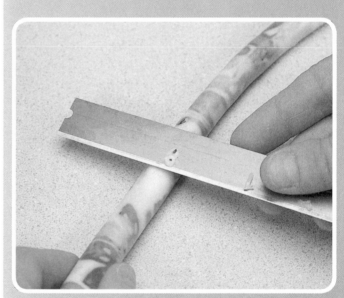
Roll Band to Remove Debris

8 Measure the length needed for the size of the bracelet (use a band of paper and measure your wrist at the widest point; tape the paper and use as guide to measure the clay band). Cut the ends at an angle and then press the seam together.

9 Stand the bracelet upright and gently roll on a hard surface to smooth the join. Bake as the manufacturer's directions instruct.

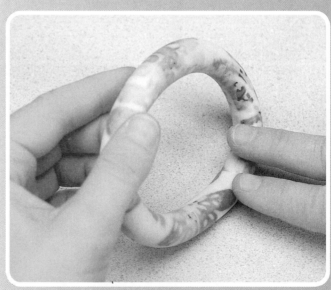
Stand Bracelet Upright and Roll

Bead Slices

These beads are great to make for a necklace or bracelet. They are quite simple to create and have a fantastic flat surface for stamping. If you want a more vibrant look, experiment by adding layers of different colors that will result in rings of color when the cane is sliced.

Must-Haves: Materials

Polymer clay: black, metallic yellow • Piece of acrylic • Polymer clay blade • Measuring tool • Collection of mini stamps • Silver pigment ink • Needle tool • Wire rod

1 Roll a log of black clay ½" in diameter. Rolling the clay under a piece of acrylic makes the rod even all around.

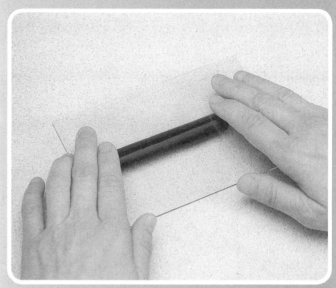

Roll Clay into Log

2 Condition and prepare a sheet of metallic yellow clay ¹/₁₆" thick and wrap it around the black log.

Wrap Yellow Clay Around Black Log

3 Slice the overlap where the wrapped clay joins. If you slightly over-wrap the clay, pull it back. The clay should have a faint impression that can serve as a guideline for slicing.

Slice Overlap

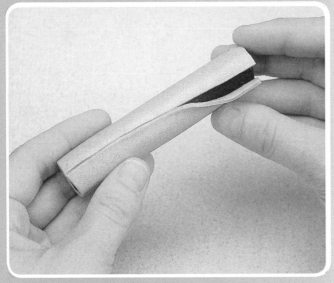

Join and Smooth Seams

4 Join and smooth the seams. Re-roll the rod to eliminate seams and, if needed, to reduce the cane. When you are making a lot of beads, work with a large diameter and reduce the cane (by rolling and stretching) it to a smaller diameter.

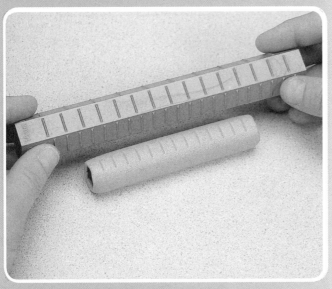

Measure Equal Amounts

5 Using your measuring tool, mark equal amounts of the cane.

Slice Through the Cane

6 Slice through the cane with a back-and-forth rolling motion as the blade cuts through the clay. This keeps the beads round.

7 Stamp the beads with inked mini stamps.

Stamp Beads

8 Pierce the beads with the needle tool. Rotate the bead and poke the hole through from the opposite side to make a smooth opening where the hole starts. Be aware of the direction of the design and how it will look on the finished necklace or bracelet.

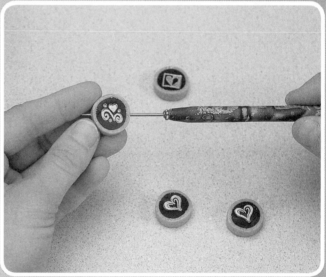

Pierce Beads

9 Place the beads on a rod for suspending during baking. The beads can also lie flat. Just be careful of the ink because it still needs to heat-set. Bake the clay as manufacturer's directions indicate.

Bake Beads

Wrist Collage

This chunky bracelet is easy and fast to make. Feel free to experiment with colored polymer clay to make a more vivid piece. The champagne and white clay used for this project gives a "wooden" look.

Must-Haves: Materials

Polymer clay: white, champagne • Pasta machine (or use a roller and wooden strips) • Paper, tape, and scissors for measuring wrist • Polymer clay blade • Set of stamps • Pigment ink: gold, black • Drill • Elastic cord

1 Combine thin sheets of the white and champagne conditioned clay (or use two colors of your choice).

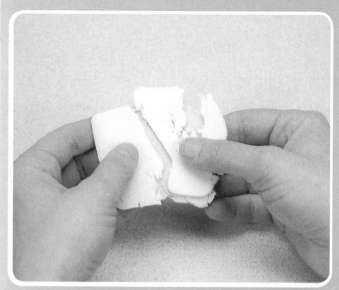

Combine Polymer Clay Sheets

2 Press the colors together through the pasta machine (or use a roller and wooden strips).

Press Colors with Pasta Machine

3 Stop when the clay is sufficiently marbled. Do not completely blend the colors.

Do Not Completely Blend Colors

Create Band to Fit Wrist

4 Create a band to fit your wrist with paper and tape.

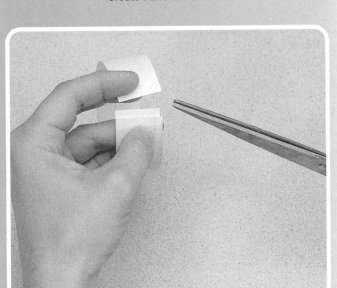

Cut Band

5 Cut the band apart.

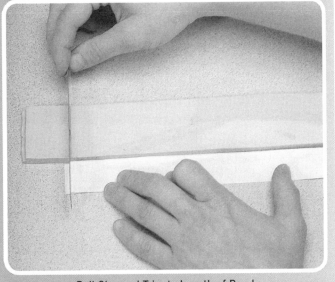

Roll Clay and Trim to Length of Band

6 Roll an even strip of clay ¼" thick, 1½" wide, and trim it to the length of the band.

7 Decorate the clay strip with a collage of images using black and gold ink. Be careful not to smear the ink. It will stay wet until it is baked.

Decorate Clay Strip

8 Cut the strip into sections 1" wide, or whatever length will accommodate equal pieces to fit within the length of the bracelet.

Cut the Strip into Sections

9 Use the side of the blade to straighten and smooth the top and bottom edges.

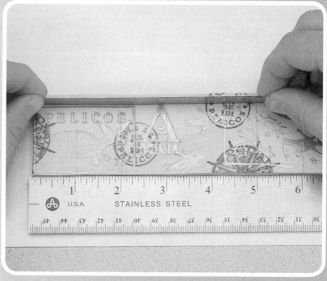

Use Blade to Straighten and Smooth

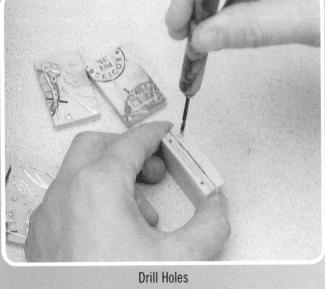
Drill Holes

10 Bake the clay as manufacturer's directions instruct. Drill holes horizontally through the sections near the top and bottom where the cord will be inserted.

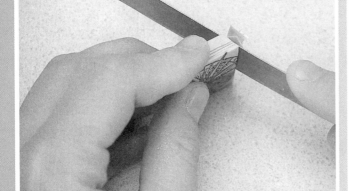
Slice Edges

11 Slice the edges, angling inward to accommodate the turn in the bracelet.

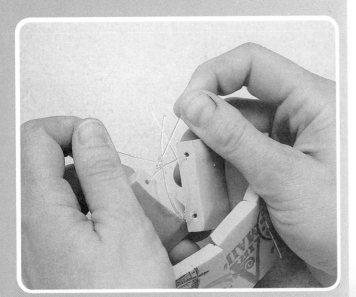
Thread Elastic and Knot

12 Thread elastic cord through the holes and secure with a knot.

Part IV

Give the Gift of Clay

Bead Charm

Here's another fun way to use scrap clay. As shown here, this is the perfect decoration for your keychain. If you prefer, incorporate the bead in a necklace or bracelet. Let your imagination guide you...

Must-Haves: Materials

Polymer clay: translucent, white • Scrap clay • Shavings from a prior project • Needle tool • Two Bali silver bead caps • Metal rod

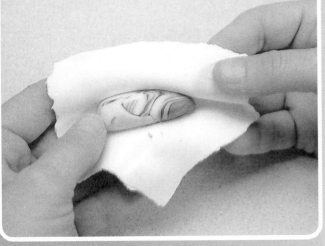

Roll Bead and Cover

1 Roll a blimp-shaped bead from scrap clay. Cover the bead with white clay.

Roll Until Smooth

2 Roll the bead until it is smooth.

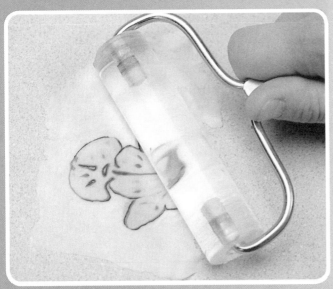

Place Shavings

3 Place the clay shavings from a prior project on an extremely thin sheet of translucent clay.

4 Cover the white bead with the translucent-embedded design. The translucent clay should be on the outside of the bead. The design should be showing through the translucent clay.

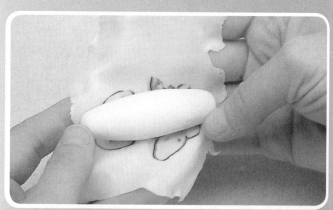

Cover Bead with Translucent-Embedded Design

5 Overlap and smooth the seams. The bead may start to take a different shape; it may start looking like a cigar.

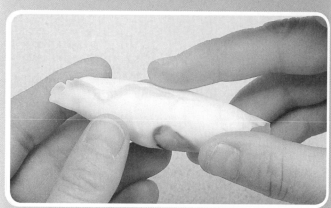

Overlap and Smooth Seams

6 Pierce a hole through each end of the bead with a needle tool.

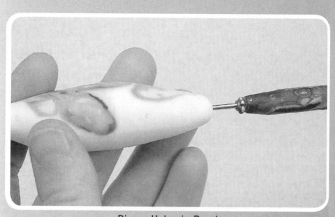

Pierce Holes in Bead

7 Place a bead cap on each end and bake on a metal rod according to the manufacturer's instructions.

Place Bead Caps on Bead and Bake

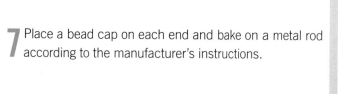

Bundle of Love

In this project, you will learn about mokume gane, the technique of stacking thin sheets of clay, distorting the layers, and cutting thin slices from the multilayered stack of clay. An adorable little decoration, this heart should be given to someone who has a strong hold on yours...

Must-Haves: Materials

Polymer Clay: transparent, transparent pink, white • Pasta machine (or use a roller and wooden strips) • Glitter • Clay tools: Polymer clay blade, NuBlade, Needle tool, Burnishing tool (you can also use the underside of a spoon for this), Stylus • One sheet of imitation silver leaf • Piece of tissue paper

1 Start with half of a 2-ounce block or ball of transparent clay. Run it through the first setting on your pasta machine. Add a small amount of glitter at a time into the clay or you will end up with a mess (fine pink glitter was used here). Sprinkle some glitter in the middle of the slab of clay and fold it in half, creating a pocket.

2 Push the sides together so that the glitter does not fall out. Leave the top open. Put this through the pasta machine with the folded end first. This way, any trapped air will discard out the opening. Repeat this several times until you have as much glitter as desired.

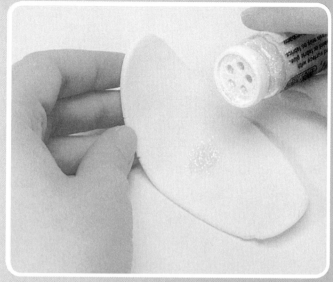

Prepare and Glitter the Clay

3 Glitter was not added to the pink half. This way, when the Skinner Blend is made, the glitter will gradually fade into the pink as it is blended. You can add glitter to both halves, however.

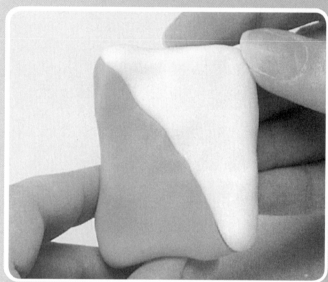

Prepare Clay for Skinner Blend

4 Run the two-toned slab of clay through the pasta machine to create the Skinner Blend.

Create Skinner Blend

Divide Clay Equally

Tips & Quips: To keep the sheet of clay from widening as it is repeatedly put through the pasta machine, place an unopened block of clay at the top of your rollers. This helps you to control the width that the clay becomes as it is repeatedly put through the rollers.

5 Cut the sheet of clay into seven equal pieces.

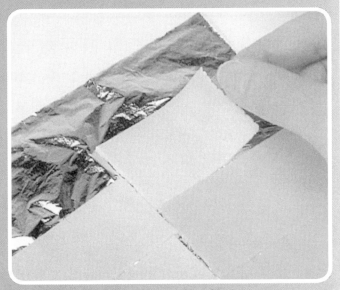

Create Mokume Gane Stack

6 Take a piece of imitation silver leaf out of the package. Be very careful with it as it comes apart very easily. Lay six pieces of clay onto the foil. Press down on them or roll over them to make sure that the leaf sticks well to the clay.

Cut and Stack Pieces

7 Cut the pieces apart again and stack them from lightest to darkest. Press them together firmly so they will stick to each other and to eliminate any air pockets.

8 Put the seventh sheet, without silver leaf, on the bottom to cover the last layer of silver. Roll a few odd-shaped balls and push them into the bottom layer. From the top it will help to create hills and valleys to take slices from, giving you a more interesting pattern.

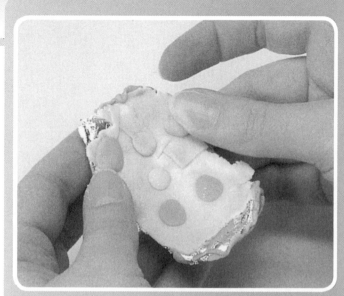

Add Odd-Shaped Balls to Bottom Layer

9 With a NuBlade, take very thin slices from the top, rotating the slab of clay as you go.

Use NuBlade to Slice

10 Form a heart shape out of scrap white clay. Begin adding the mokume gane slices until the entire heart is covered.

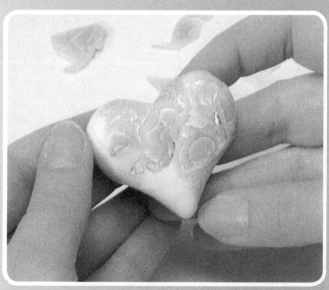

Form Heart

Place Tissue Paper and Smooth

11 Once the heart is covered, place a piece of tissue paper over it and use a burnishing tool or the back of a spoon to rub all of the slices down for a smooth surface.

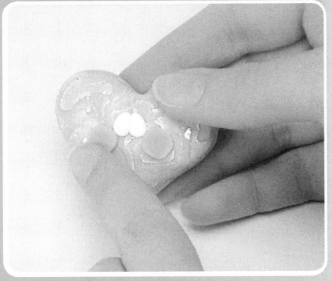

Create Heart's Face

12 Place white clay eyes next to each other on the heart. The cheeks are made from leftover Skinner Blend rolled into a cane from a dark center to a light edge. Two slices from this cane create the cheeks. Place each below the eyes and slightly off to the side.

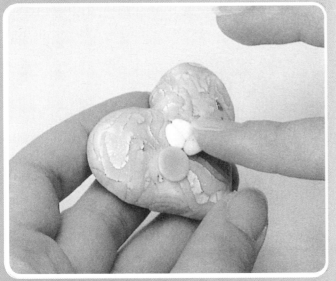

Create Nose

13 The nose is a small ball of the pink transparent placed directly under the eyes.

14 Press the needle tool into the clay starting at one cheek and pull it through the clay to the other side to form a mouth.

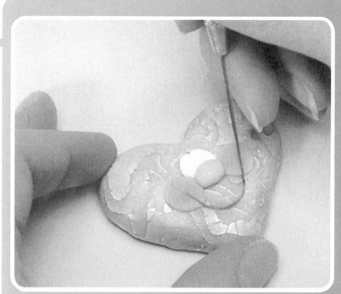

Form Mouth

15 Use the wide end of the stylus to create dimples at the corners of the mouth. Also use the stylus to gently pull the mouth open.

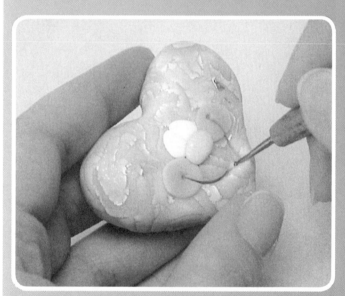

Add Dimples and Pull Mouth Down

16 Make a small teardrop of pink transparent clay for the tongue. Use the needle tool to insert it into his mouth.

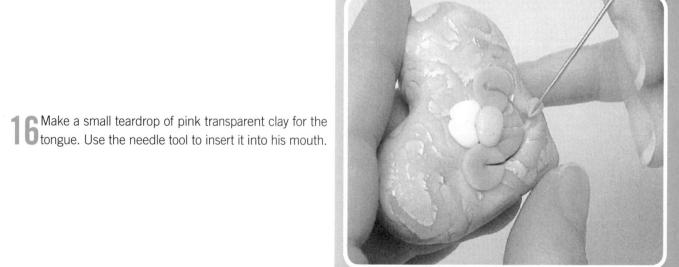

Create Tongue

In the Name of L-O-V-E Magnets

This card is perfect to give to the one you love. Those who receive this card can detach the letter magnets and put them on the refrigerator to remind them that they're cherished.

Must-Haves: Materials

1 block polymer clay: black, gold • Pasta machine (or use a roller and wooden strips) • Automotive protectant • L-O-V-E rubber stamp set • Craft knife • Eyeshadow applicator (optional) • Gold pearlized powder • Superglue • Cooling surface (tile) • 11"×5½" black cardstock (and a scoring tool) • Double-sided adhesive • 5"×5" piece of gold crinkle paper • 4½"×4½" gold scallop paper • Decorative edging scissors • Cotton swabs and water • 4"×4" white mulberry paper with gold flecks • Adhesive-backed magnetic sheeting • Magnets • Matte acrylic spray sealer • Poster tack

1 Roll out the black clay on the third-largest setting of the pasta machine. Lightly spray the clay with automotive protectant and spread it with your fingers.

2 Stamp the L-O-V-E letters into the clay. Cut out the letter squares along the stamped markings with a craft knife. Remove any excess clay.

Roll out Clay, Stamp, and Cut out Letter Squares

3 With either the tip of your finger or an eye shadow applicator, apply gold pearlized powder on the raised area of the stamped letters.

Add Gold Details

4 Roll ⅛ block of gold clay into a 5" log and run it through the pasta machine (or use a roller and wooden strips) on the fourth-largest setting.

5 Trim the clay sheet to 5"×1" with a clay blade. Cut four strips ⅛" wide and twist.

Create Twist Border

Glue Border to Letters

6 Brush superglue along one side of each letter and gently press the twisted strip against the clay's edge. Continue gluing the border around the entire letter, wrapping all four sides.

7 Trim the excess clay with a craft knife. Repeat this step for the remaining three letters. Bake the letters at 270°F for twenty-five minutes, then let cool on a tile.

Create Card Background

8 While the letters are in the oven, score and fold the 11"×5½" sheet of black cardstock in half. Apply double-sided adhesive to the 5"×5" piece of gold crinkle paper and attach it to the cardstock.

Add Scalloped-Edged Paper

9 Trim a piece of gold scallop-pattern paper with decorative edging scissors to 4½"×4½". Apply double-sided adhesive and center it over the gold crinkle paper.

Continues ➡

10 Dip a cotton swab into water. Wet the outer edges of the 4"×4" mulberry paper with the dampened swab.

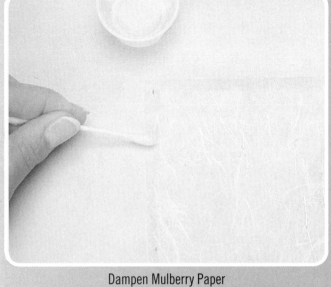

Dampen Mulberry Paper

11 Gently grasp the mulberry paper in one hand. Tear away the dampened edges of the paper. This will leave a feathered edge.

Create Feathered Edge

12 Apply double-sided adhesive to one side of the feathered paper. Center the mulberry paper and place it on top of the scallop paper.

Add Mulberry Paper to Card

Add Magnetic Sheeting to Letters

13 Loosen the cooled letters from the tile with a clay blade. Cut four $^7/_8$"×$^7/_8$" squares from an adhesive-backed magnetic sheet. Peel off the adhesive backing and superglue them to the adhesive side for extra hold.

14 Press the magnets onto the back of each letter. Lightly spray the letters with the acrylic spray sealer to secure the powder, and let them dry.

Apply Poster Tack to Letters

15 Apply a small ball of poster tack to the back of each letter. Arrange the letters on the mulberry paper as shown on the finished card.

Tips & Quips: Send polymer clay cards in padded envelopes. Mark both sides of the envelope, "Please Hand Cancel." Automated canceling may damage the card.

Cute as a Button

Take your favorite stamp and create your very own buttons! Perfect to use as decoration for other projects, too. These are easy and fun to make!

Must-Haves: Materials

Black polymer clay • PearlEx gold powder • Rubber stamp • Polymer clay blade • 600-grit sandpaper (wet) • Button backs • Superglue

Condition and Prepare Clay

1 Condition and prepare a sheet of clay ⅛" thick and large enough to impress the stamped design.

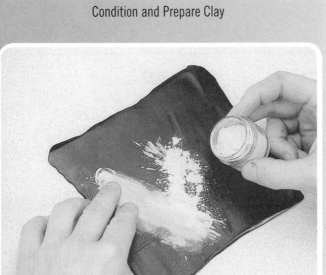

Coat Clay

2 Coat the clay with gold powder.

Stamp Clay

3 Stamp the image firmly into the clay.

Continues ➤

Divide Design

4 Using a polymer clay blade, divide the design into squares. Bake as the manufacturer's directions instruct.

Rub Button on Wet Sandpaper

5 Face the button down and rub gently against wet sandpaper to remove the gold on the raised design. Do not sand too much or you will remove the entire design.

Glue Button Backs

6 Glue the button backs on with superglue.

Hearty Wire Holder

PAGE 138

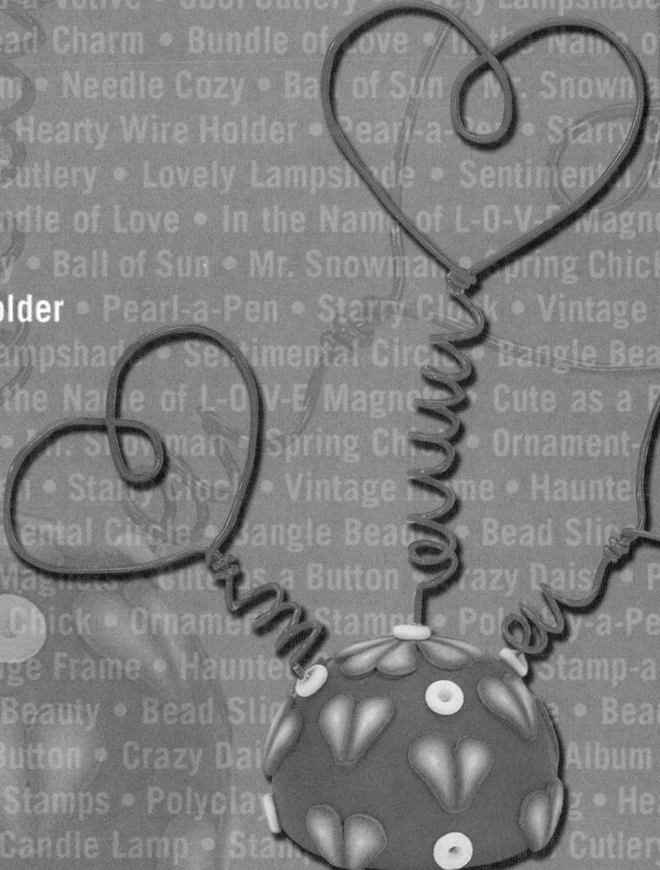

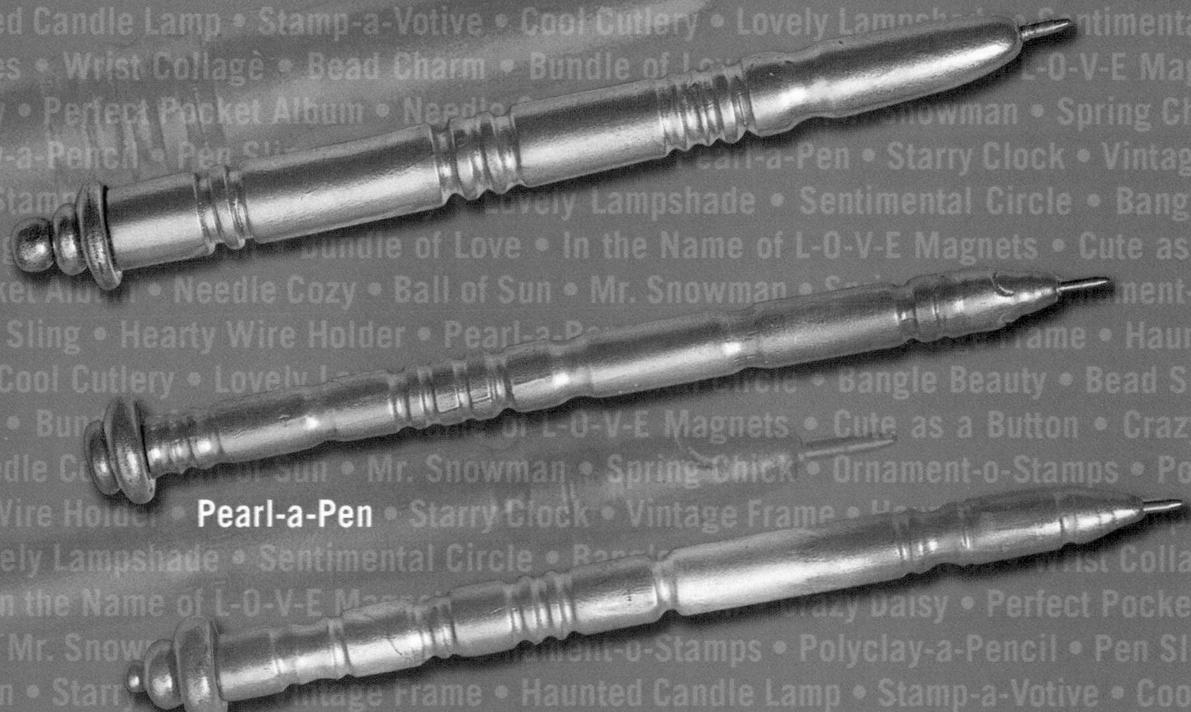

Pearl-a-Pen

PAGE 143

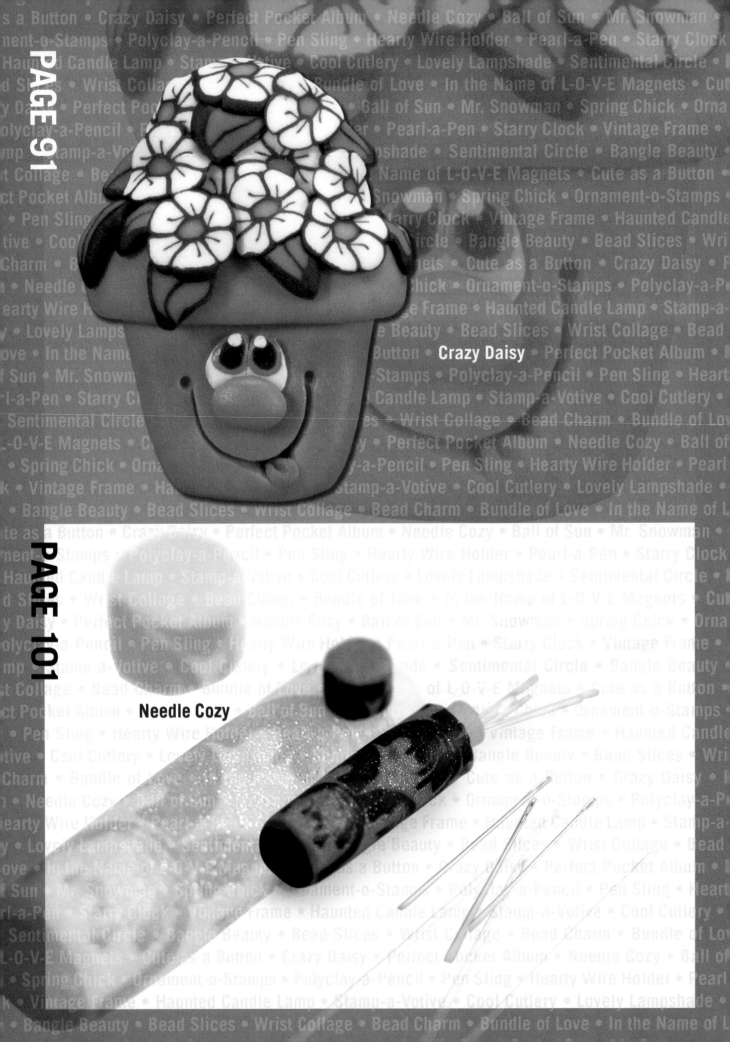

Crazy Daisy

Needle Cozy

Perfect Pocket Album

Spring Chick

Ball of Sun

Mr. Snowman

Ornament-o-Stamps

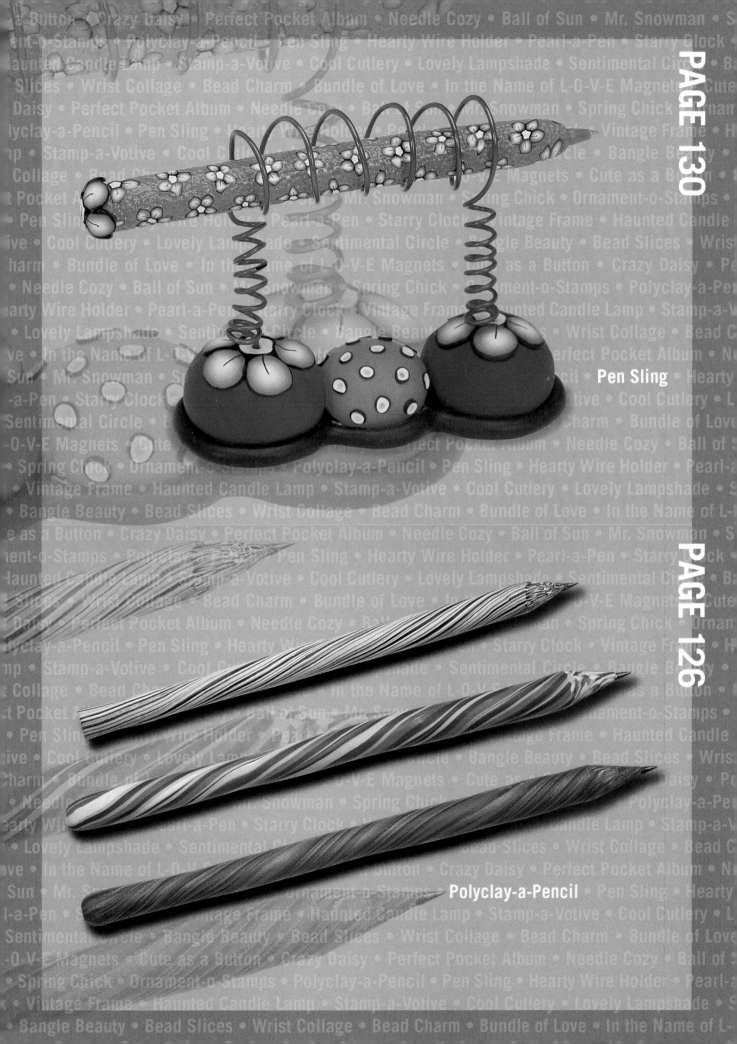

PAGE 130

Pen Sling

PAGE 126

Polyclay-a-Pencil

Cute as a Button

Crazy Daisy

This tiny flowerpot is perfect to create for a barren shelf or window-sill—no watering necessary!

Must-Haves: Materials

Polymer clay: white, yellow, green, black, terra cotta, pink • NuBlade or craft knife • Pasta machine (or use a roller and wooden strips)

1 To make a simple leaf cane, start by rolling a $^7/_8$" ball of green clay into a $2^1/_2$" long by $^7/_{16}$" wide log. Use the NuBlade to divide the log in half vertically.

2 Roll a sheet of black clay through the #5 setting on the pasta machine (see page 5 for the pasta machine setting equivalents if you are using a roller).

3 Lay one half of the log on the black sheet, flat side down. Press on the top of the green gently so the black sheet will stick to it. Use the knife or NuBlade to trim the black clay around the green log.

4 Place the half of the log with the black sheet on it on top of the other half. Refer to the photo for guidance. You should now have a log with a black stripe down the center of it.

Start Creating Leaf Cane

5 Cut a straight edge on the remaining black sheet. Lay the green log at the edge of the sheet. Roll the log in the sheet, being careful not to overlap the black. Watch out for air bubbles.

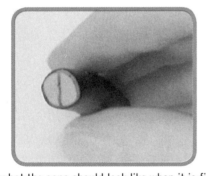

This is what the cane should look like when it is finished. Do not be discouraged if the end looks a little distorted at first. Once you slice off a piece from the end, you will have a better idea of what the rest of the cane really looks like.

6 To make the flower petals, repeat the steps for the leaf cane, using a $^7/_8$" ball of white rolled clay into a $2^1/_2$"×$^7/_{16}$" wide log. Instead of making the center black sheet of clay go all the way across, make it go only halfway. Also make a yellow cane that is just a $^5/_8$" yellow ball of clay made into a 1"×$^3/_8$" wide log, then wrap it in black clay. Don't add a line in the center of this one.

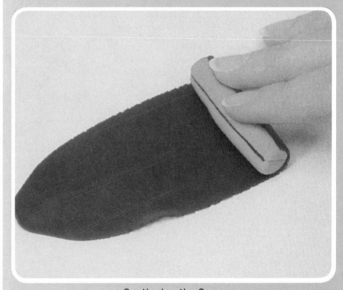

Continuing the Cane

Create Flower Cane

Reduce Cane Sizes

7 Reduce the flower petal cane to $^3/_{16}$" in diameter by gently rolling it on the table. Cut six $1^1/_2$" long pieces. Reduce the yellow cane to the same size and cut one piece $1^1/_2$" long.

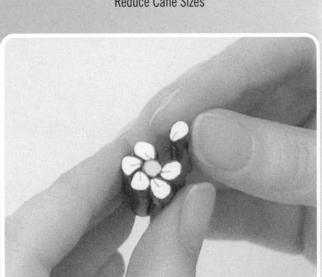

Cane Assembly

8 Assemble the flower petal canes around the yellow middle. Make sure that the black line in the petal is on the inside next to the yellow center on all of the pieces. Also check to make sure that they are that way at the other end too. Sometimes when a cane is being reduced, it can get turned around in the middle.

Stretch Cane

9 Because you'll want to maintain the shape of the petals, do not roll the cane on the table to reduce it. (That would result in a round cane instead of a flower-shaped edge.) Instead, gently and slowly stretch the cane. Use both hands to keep turning the piece as you stretch.

10 The flowerpot is made from a $^3/_4$" ball of terra cotta clay. Form the shape of a plant pot. At the top of the pot, pull a small amount of clay upward. This will be where the cane slices are added.

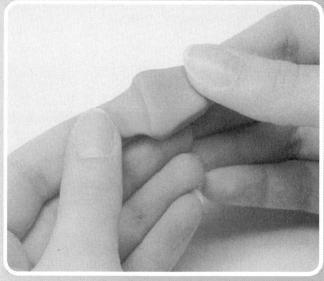

Create Flowerpot

11 Make the brim of the flowerpot from a $^7/_{16}$" terra cotta ball rolled out to a $1^1/_2$" long log and slightly flatten it with your finger.

12 Attach the brim starting at one side and then wrapping it around to the other side.

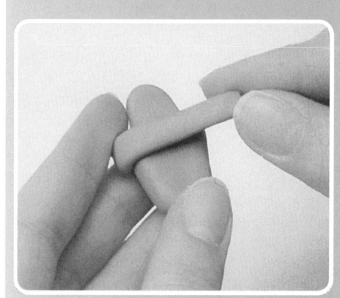

Create and Attach Brim

13 If the top part that was pulled from the pot is a little too flat to add the flower slices, add a small ball of terra cotta clay and flatten it slightly. Add his face.

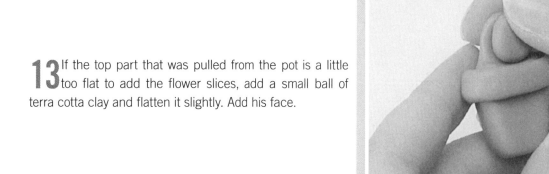

Add Face

Place Flowers

14 Before slicing any of the leaf cane, pinch one side to shape it into a leaf. This is much easier to do before you cut it, but it can also be done after. Begin placing flower slices and leaf slices all over the extra clay at the top of the pot.

Finish and Bake

15 Crazy Daisy is ready to bake when you are satisfied with how the flowers are arranged.

Perfect Pocket Album

Perfect for slipping in a purse or bag—or in your pocket—this mini photo album is a great way to keep collected and cherished photos at hand.

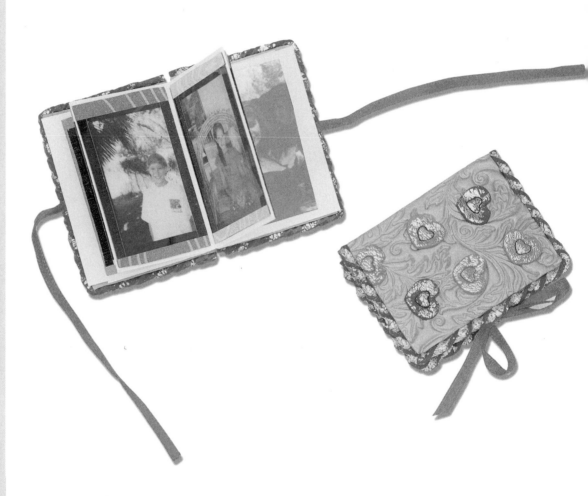

Must-Haves: Materials

Polymer clay, 1 block: gold, purple, turquoise, fuchsia • Pasta machine (or use a roller and wooden strips) • Automotive protectant • Leaf pattern rubber stamp • Clay blade • Gold leaf foil • Small and medium heart pattern cutters • Superglue • Knitting needle • White cardstock (and scoring tool) • Double-sided carpet tape • Scissors • 2 pieces of $1/8$" purple satin ribbon, 5" long

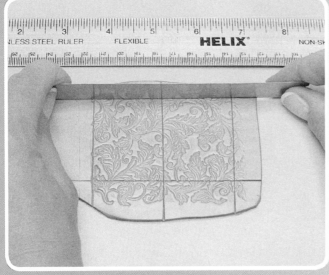

Create Book Cover

1 Roll $^1/_3$ block of gold clay through the third-largest setting on the pasta machine (or use a roller and wooden strips). Spray automotive protectant on the clay sheet and spread it with your fingers.

2 Stamp the clay sheet with the leaf stamp. Cut two $1^1/_2$"×2" covers from the stamped clay with a clay blade.

Create Foiled Hearts

3 Roll large balls of purple, turquoise, and fuchsia clay through the largest setting of the pasta machine. Tear bits of gold leaf foil and apply them over the flattened clay.

4 Run the foiled clays through the fourth-largest setting of the pasta machine. Punch out six hearts, two of each color, using the medium heart pattern cutter.

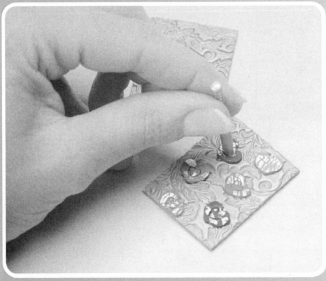

Glue Hearts to Front Cover

5 Superglue the hearts onto one of the stamped covers. Press the center of each heart with the small pattern cutter.

Continues

6 Roll ⅛ block of purple clay into a 6" log. Roll the log lengthwise through largest setting of the pasta machine. Apply a piece of gold leaf over the flattened clay.

7 Run the clay lengthwise through the fifth-largest setting of the pasta machine. Cut two 6"×⅛" strips from the foiled purple clay with a clay blade. Twist both strips along their entire length.

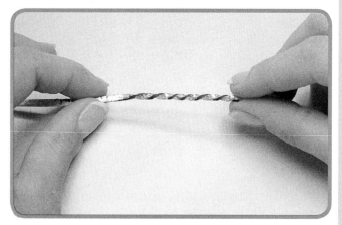

Create Twisted Border

8 Superglue the twisted strips around three sides of each cover: two short sides and one long side. Press a knitting needle against the indented sections along the twist to secure. Bake the panels at 270°F for twenty-five minutes.

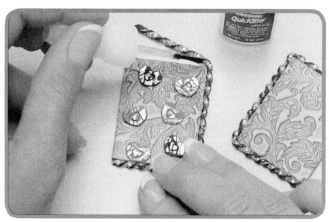

Add Twisted Border to Book Covers

9 Cut a 1⅞"×8" strip of white cardstock. Following the lines on the template on the template to the right, score the cardstock.

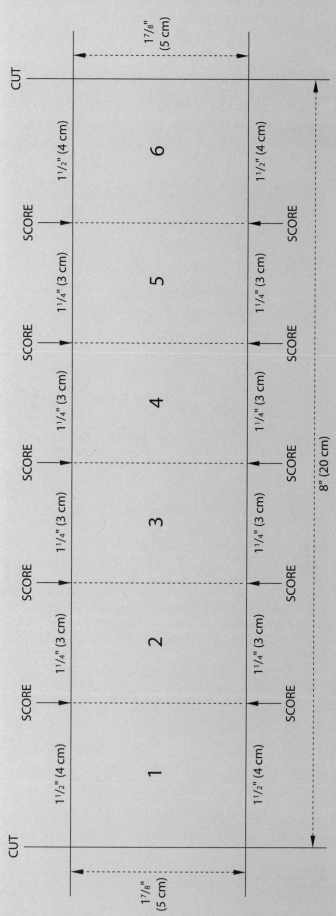

Create Pages of Album

10 Fold the cardstock along the score lines, accordion style. You should have five score lines and six panels.

Add Double-Sided Tape

11 Cut four squares from a roll of double-sided carpet tape with scissors. Place one square on panels 1, 2, 4, and 6. Remove the tape backing from panels 2 and 4.

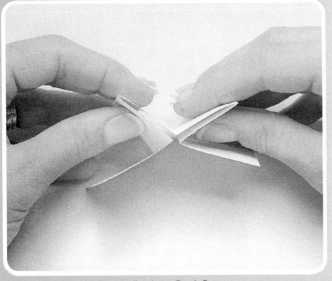

Create Back-to-Back Pages

12 Fold panel 3 onto the exposed adhesive of panel 2. Fold panel 5 onto the exposed adhesive of panel 4.

13 When the clay panels have cooled, remove the tape backing from panels 1 and 6.

14 Press one 5" piece of ribbon halfway over the tape on panel 1 and press another 5" piece of ribbon halfway over the tape on panel 6.

Assemble Book

15 Make sure that the spine of the album is flush with the untrimmed edges of each panel and that the ribbon protrudes from the middle of the long-trimmed edge. If the pages are not properly aligned, the book may not open correctly.

16 Select six photos and trim them to fit inside the album. Attach the photos to each page with a piece of carpet tape.

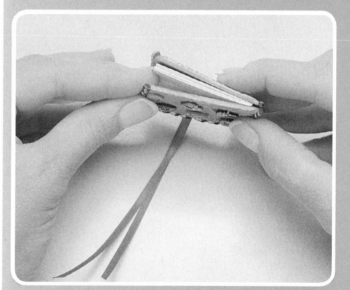

Add Finishing Touches

Needle Cozy

You can cover any object you like with mokume gane—like a needle case! Feel free to use whatever is lying around, including your own clay tools. You'll soon find how fun and easy it is to experiment with this exciting technique!

Must-Haves: Materials

Polymer clay: 1 block—metallic silver polymer clay, 1/8 block yellow polymer clay mixed to yield pastel lime clay, metallic blue and metallic red mixed in equal parts to yield purple clay • Roller • Cornstarch • Rubber stamps • Polymer clay blade • Wooden needle case • Tacky glue

1 Begin by rolling a sheet of pastel lime about $^3/_{32}$" thick. Prepare another sheet of green clay to "catch" the pieces sliced in the process. Set the second sheet aside.

2 Prepare a sheet of purple clay as thin as possible, about $^1/_{64}$" (less than half a millimeter). Stack the purple layer on top of one of the lime sheets and smooth with roller.

Stack Purple Clay on Lime Clay and Smooth

3 Dust clay with cornstarch and impress the stamp into the clay—a deep impression is crucial.

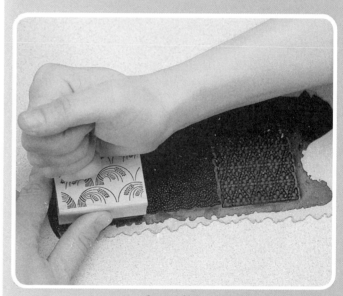

Stamp Clay

4 Use the flexible blade to slice an extremely thin layer from the stacked clay. The design in the stamp will emerge as the top layer is removed.

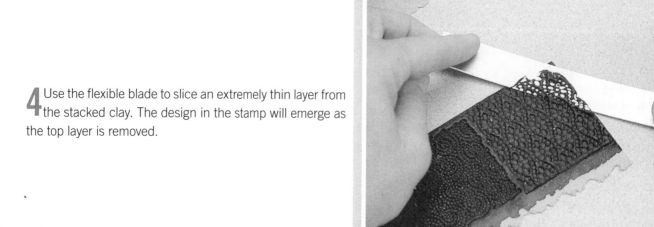

Use Blade to Slice Thin Layer

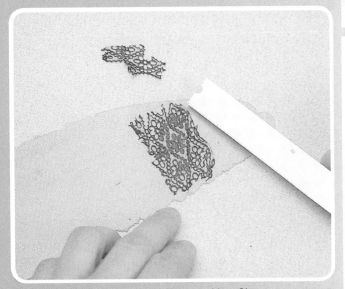

Place Removed Slices on Lime Clay

5 Place the removed slices on the sheet of lime clay set aside. This is not scrap and will later be used to cover beads. Set aside.

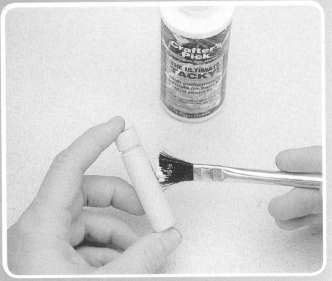

Coat Case with Glue

6 Coat the wooden needle case with glue. Set aside to dry.

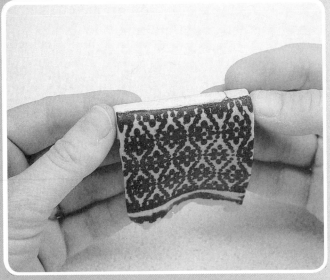

Cut Clay Rectangle and Release Air Pockets

7 From your mokume gane stack, cut a rectangle of clay wide and long enough to wrap the needle case. Release any air pockets by making a small slice sideways into the pocket and smoothing the clay into place as the air is released.

Continues

8 Slice vertically where the clay overlaps and carefully smooth the seam.

Slice Vertically

9 Slice the indent where the cap meets the body of the needle case.

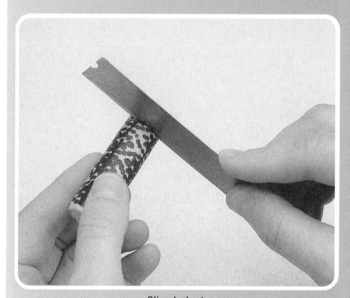

Slice Indent

10 Remove any excess clay from the top and bottom of the needle case.

Remove Excess Clay

Place Top and Bottom of Case on Lime Clay and Cut

11 Place the top and bottom of the case on the lime clay and cut along the edge.

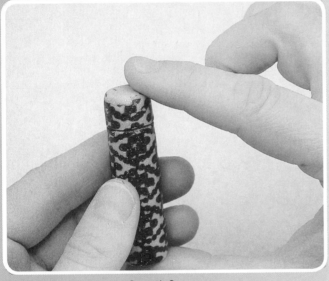

Smooth Seams

12 Smooth the seams along the top and bottom edges. Bake the whole piece according to the manufacturer's directions.

Ball of Sun

Brighten up someone's day—perhaps someone you haven't seen in a while—with this cheery sun. This spectacular cane was developed by Donna Kato. For other interesting variations you can also try this technique with plain transparent clay and leaf, adding the thin slices to a colored background.

Must-Haves: Materials

Polymer clay: transparent yellow, transparent orange, white, pink • Pasta machine (or use a roller and wooden strips) • Imitation gold leaf • NuBlade • Blush • Makeup brush

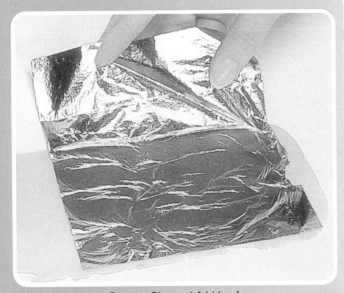

Prepare Clay and Add Leaf

1 Make a Skinner Blend with a 2-ounce block each of yellow and orange transparent clay (see page 17 for more on Skinner Blend). Run through a pasta machine on the fourth setting. Place a piece or two of imitation gold leaf on the sheet of clay and gently pat down the leaf so that it sticks to the clay.

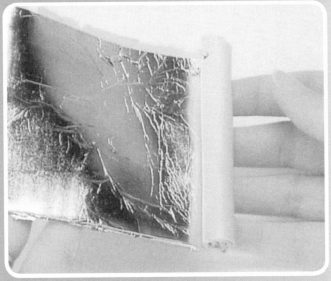

Roll Clay and Leaf

2 Tightly roll the sheet of clay and the gold leaf together.

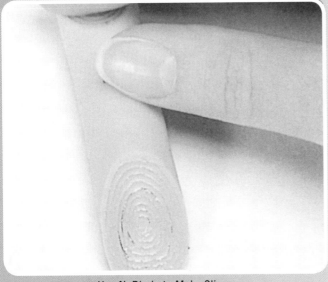

Use NuBlade to Make Slices

3 Use a new NuBlade to make steep slices from the cane. Make them as thin as possible.

Continues

4 Cut out a sun shape from transparent yellow clay that has been run through the first setting on the pasta machine. Begin laying cane slices all over the top of the sunrays. When the piece is covered, lay a piece of tissue paper over the rays and burnish the surface until it is flat and even.

Create Rays

5 Make a ⁷⁄₈" ball of marbled transparent yellow and orange clay. Place it in the center of the sunrays and gently press down on the sides of the ball. Use clay to create the face and brush blush onto the cheeks.

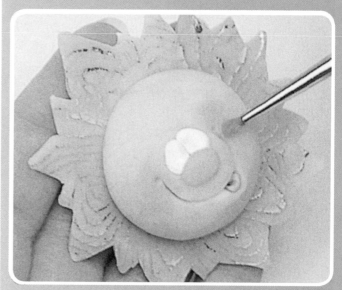

Create Face

Mr. Snowman

Mr. Snowman is a cheerful character who can be detached from this card to brighten any tree or holiday display. Not just another card to be taped to the door, this festive decoration is sure to be found hanging on a tree throughout the entire holiday season.

Must-Haves: Materials

1 block polymer clay: black, green, white, red, yellow, orange • Pasta machine (or use a roller and wooden strips) • Tracing paper • Craft knife • Scouring pad • Pink blush • Eye shadow applicator • Needle tool • Small star pattern cutter • Ball-tip stylus • 18" green plastic-coated craft wire • Needle-nose pliers • Large-gauge knitting needle • 7"×11" piece of gold cardstock • Decorative edge scissors • 5"×6½"" piece of holly-pattern paper • 5"×6" piece of red mulberry paper with gold flecks • Double-sided adhesive • Poster tack • Cotton swabs

1 Roll out a block of white clay on the largest setting of your pasta machine (or use a roller and wooden strips) and, using the template on the left and a craft knife, create the snowman.

Add Texture and Blush

2 Pat a kitchen scouring pad over the surface of the snowman to texture it. Apply dots of blush to the snowman's cheeks with an eye shadow applicator.

3 Roll a ⅝" ball of black clay into a 1⅛" log. Flatten and shape the log into a "scrunchy" rectangle with your fingers to create a crown. Press the crown over the top edge of the head.

Create Tophat

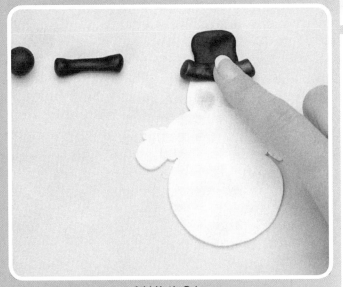

Add Hat's Brim

4 Roll a ⁵⁄₈" ball of black clay into a 1¹⁄₈" log. Slightly flatten the log and indent the center with your fingertips to make the brim of the hat. Press the brim over the base of the crown.

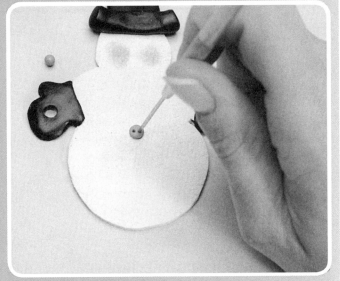

Create Mittens and Buttons

5 Roll ¹⁄₈ of a block of black clay through the third-largest setting of a pasta machine (or use a roller and wooden strips) and cut out the mittens that you traced from the template above.

6 Use a needle tool to make holes in the center of each mitten. Roll two pinches of green clay into tiny balls for buttons and press them onto the center of the snowman's torso.

7 Slightly flatten the balls with your fingertips. Poke two holes into the center of each button with a needle tool.

Create Candy Cane

8 Roll pinches of white and red clay into very thin logs (work with the white first). Clean your hands thoroughly after using the red clay. Twist the logs together. Roll them against the work surface until they are smooth and ¹⁄₈" in diameter.

9 Bend the top 1" of the candy cane into a hook and press it onto the hat, above the brim.

Continues

10 Roll a pinch of yellow clay through the fifth-largest setting of the pasta machine (or use a roller with wooden strips). Cut out a star with the pattern cutter. Press the star over the bottom of the candy cane to secure it to the hat.

Add Gold Star

11 Roll $1/8$ block of black and $1/8$ block of red clay through the largest setting of the pasta machine (or use a roller and wooden strips). Stack the clay sheets and trim with a clay blade to make a 1"×1" square.

12 Roll the square through the third-largest setting of the pasta machine. Cut this sheet in half and stack the halves together, alternating colors. Roll $1/16$ block of red clay through the fifth-largest setting of the pasta machine.

13 Cut six $1/8$" slices from the stack. Lay these slices, side-by-side, over the red clay sheet. Run this sheet, stripes facing up, through the fourth-largest setting of the pasta machine. Cut two 2"×$1/4$" strips from the striped sheet.

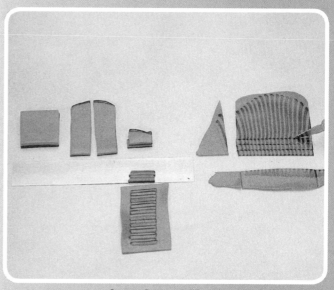

Create Patterned Scarf

14 Wrap the first striped strip around the snowman's neck and cut the excess away. Fold the second strip at a right angle. Place the folded strip over the right side of the scarf to form the tails. Trim scarf tails at an angle with a craft knife.

Add Scarf to Snowman

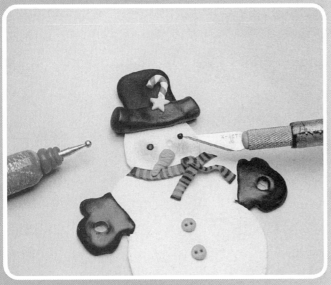

Add Nose and Eyes

15 Roll a pinch of orange clay into a long teardrop. Bend the teardrop with your fingers to create a crooked carrot. Place the carrot, pointed end down, at an angle between the cheeks:

16 Mark lines along the length of the carrot with the tip of the craft knife. Make two indentations over the cheeks with a ball-tip stylus. Roll two tiny pinches of black clay into balls. Press the balls into the holes. Bake the snowman at 270°F for thirty minutes.

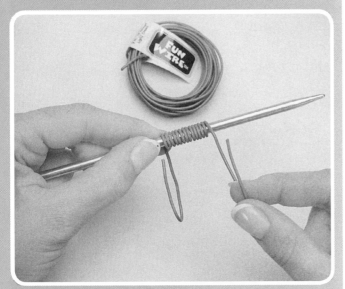

Coil Wire

17 Allow the snowman to cool completely. Bend the 18" piece of green wire in half over a large knitting needle. Wrap each end around the knitting needle six times (for a total of twelve coils).

18 Bend the remaining lengths of wire in half to form a long "U" shape. Slide the wire off the knitting needle. Holding the wire coiled at both ends, slightly pull it apart with your fingers and bend it in an arch.

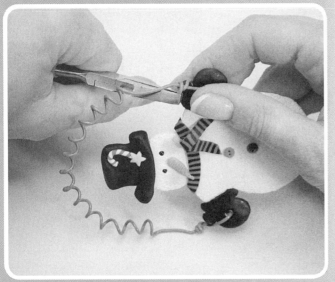

Add Wire to Snowman

19 Slip the "U" shaped hooks through the mitten holes. With needle-nose pliers, twist the ends of each wire two to three times around the wire extending from the coil.

20 Fold a piece of gold cardstock in half and trim the top and bottom edges with decorative edging scissors, creating a $5^1/_2$"×7" card. Trim the holly-pattern paper with decorative edging scissors to 5"×$6^1/_4$".

21 Create an outline of the snowman by feathering the edge of the mulberry paper, about $^1/_2$" from the edge of the snowman (see page 83 from the In the Name of L-O-V-E Magnets to learn more about feathering). Attach these three pieces with double-sided adhesive to make the card.

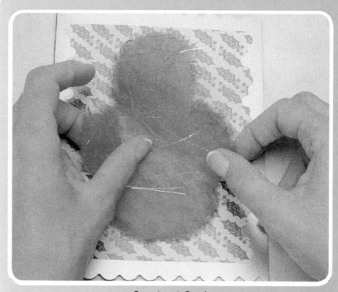

Construct Card

22 Apply four to five small balls of poster tack to the back of the snowman. Press the snowman over the center of the mulberry paper to secure the ornament to the card.

Attach Ornament to Card

Spring Chick

Here's a neat little project to make in honor of spring. For Easter, you could make just the egg—in different colors—and put them in a cute wicker basket for decoration.

Inclusions

Inclusions such as the crayons used in this project can be varied when using with transparent or opaque clay. Here are some ideas for what you can mix in with your transparent or opaque clays:

- Glitter
- Shavings from pastels
- Spices
- Colored sand
- Dried flowers
- Potpourri

Must-Haves: Materials

Polymer clay: transparent, yellow, white, orange • Crayons: pink, purple • Pasta machine (or use a roller and wooden strips) • Craft knife • Stylus • Two matching yellow feathers • Superglue

1 Chop small, fine pieces of pink and purple crayons on a note card.

Prepare Clay

2 Flatten a ¾" ball of transparent clay. Slowly add the crayon pieces to the transparent clay.

Add Crayon Pieces

3 To mix together, fold clay in half to create a pocket. Run this through the pasta machine (or use a roller and wooden strips) with the folded end touching the rollers first. Roll through a few times and then add more of the crayon.

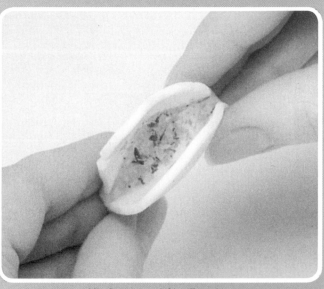

Mix Crayon and Clay Together

Create Zigzag

4 Once all the crayon is added to the transparent clay, form the clay into an egg shape and cut a zigzag edge toward the top of the egg.

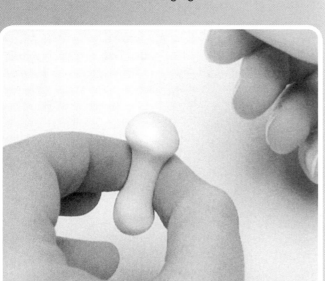

Create Chick's Body

5 Make the chick from a ¾" ball of yellow clay. Place the ball between your fingers and roll half of the ball into a log. The top, rounded end will be his head.

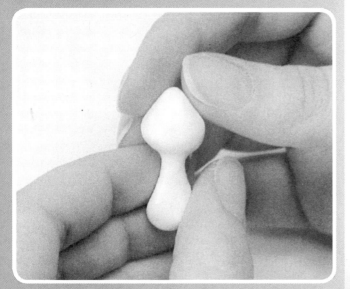

Define Head and Body

6 Flatten the rounded end slightly and shape it into a rounded triangle. This will be his head, and the other half will be the lower portion of his body.

7 Flatten his body, but not the head, more and press it into the back side of the egg so that the neck and head are above the zigzag cut edge.

Attach Body to Egg

8 Lay the egg on your work surface, front side up, and press the edge down so that the back will be flat.

9 Make the chick's eyes from a $1/8$" ball of white clay and add them to the head.

10 Make the beak from a $1/4$" ball of orange clay. Use both hands and rock it back and forth between your fingers and thumbs. Essentially, you will be making an elongated diamond shape.

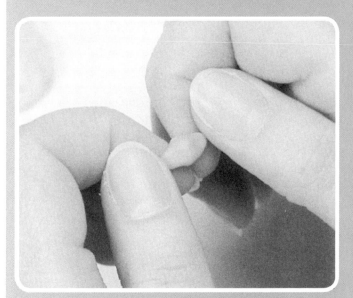

Create Beak

11 Slightly pinch the sides of the diamond to form the corners of the beak.

Pinch Beak

Secure Beak to Chick's Face

12 Place the beak just below his eyes. Only press down on the sides of the beak to secure it to his face.

Create the Mouth

13 Use a scalpel or knife to cut open his beak and create his mouth. Cut a line from one side to the other, leaving a majority of the clay on the top part of the beak.

Create Dimples

14 Use the stylus to add his dimples.

Open up Mouth

15 Use the stylus to open up his mouth slightly by inserting it into the center of the opening and pulling the clay down a bit.

Flatten Beak Slightly

16 Use the side of the stylus to slightly flatten the beak's lower half.

Attach Feathers

17 Cut the feathers to fit the size of the chick. Each feather should not stick out more than 1" from each side of the chick, unless that is how you want it to look.

18 Add a little white glue to the end of one feather and gently press it into his neck, being very careful not to go all the way through. Repeat on the other side.

19 Refer to page 14 to detail the eyes.

Ornament-o-Stamps

This project is easy to make. All you need is some clay, a few stamps, and something to use to hang the ornament. The beveled edge and a cleanly drilled hole add elegance. Use metallic ink for a classic look.

Must-Haves: Materials

White polymer clay • Holiday stamps of your choice • Three colors of metallic pigment ink • Polymer clay blade • Drill tool or drill bit • 12" metallic elastic cording

1 Condition the clay (see page 6 on how to condition) and prepare a slab about $^3/_{16}$" thick, large enough to stamp the image and allow for a $^1/_8$" border.

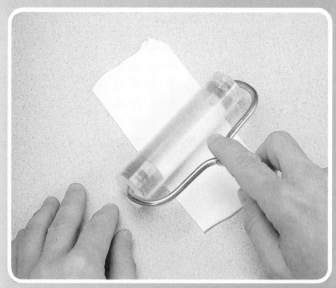

Condition Clay

2 Since the clay is white, it may pick up dust or hair. Clean the surface of the clay by dragging a blade gently over the top of the slab, removing the top layer and clearing it completely of debris. Remove the clay from the blade by pulling it off with a mound of scrap clay. Do not remove it with your fingers.

Remove Debris from Clay

3 Ink one portion of the stamp with a color of pigment ink.

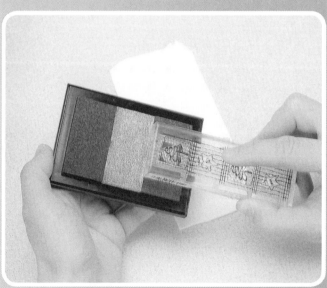

Ink a Portion of the Stamp

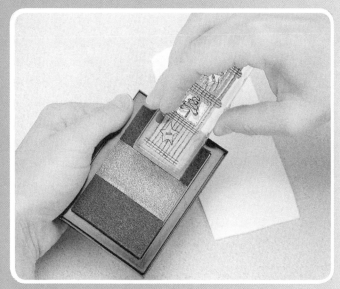

Ink Remainder of Stamp

4 Ink the remainder of the stamp in other colors. Do not saturate the stamp with ink. Only the lines of the image should bear ink.

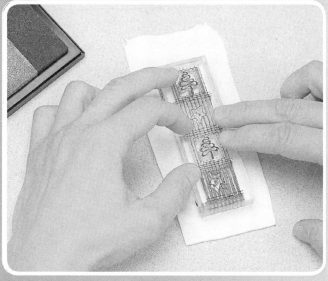

Press Stamp

5 Press the stamp firmly into the clay and pull straight out. Since the clay will be baked, the pigment will bind to the clay. However, the pigment will smear if you touch it before it is baked, so be very careful once you have stamped the clay.

Bevel Edges

6 Bevel the edges of the design by cutting the clay with the blade at a slant.

Continues

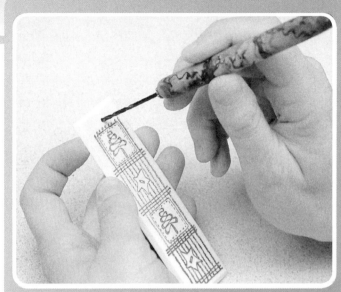

7 Bake as the manufacturer's directions indicate. When the piece is cool, drill a hole though the top center of the ornament with a drill tool or a drill bit.

Drill Hole

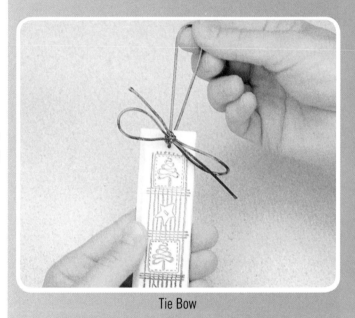

8 Thread a 12" length of cord through the hole and tie into a bow. Slip the bow into the hole, creating a loop to hang the ornament.

Tie Bow

Part V

Dress Your Desk!

Polyclay-a-Pencil
Pen Sling
Hearty Wire Holder
Pearl-a-Pen

Polyclay-a-Pencil

Polymer clay pencils are fun to make and they can be sharpened like ordinary pencils. Use a strong clay for this project, and do not make the pencils too thin or they will easily bend and snap!

Must-Haves: Materials

Small quantities of polymer clay in two or more colors for marbling (the equivalent of about half a 2-ounce block of clay per pencil) • Craft knife • 2mm-thick clutch pencil lead • Pencil sharpener for wide pencils • Tile for smoothing (optional)

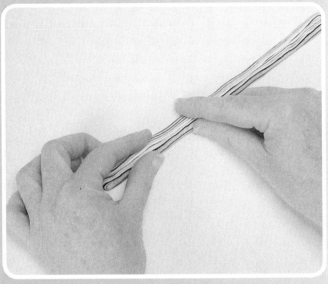

Create Marbled Log

1 Marble the different colored clays together, keeping the streaks parallel, until all the streaks are thin but still distinct (see page 21 for the Marbling technique).

2 Form into a log about ½" in diameter and 8" long.

3 Press the log down on your work surface to give it a semi-circular cross section all along its length.

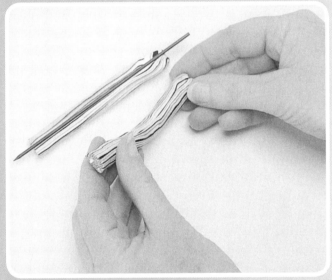

Add Pencil Lead

4 Cut the log in half and turn one half so that the flat side is facing up.

5 Lay the pencil lead centrally along this side (flat side up) and then cover it with the other half, flat side down, to sandwich the lead in the middle of the log. Note that one end of the led is pointed—this will be the end to sharpen.

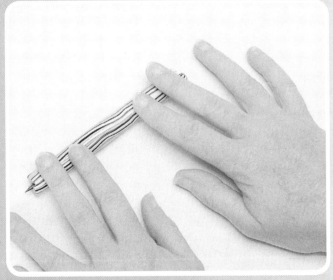

Reform Log

6 Press the two pieces together to make a log, but be careful not to break the lead inside the clay.

7 Roll the log on your work surface to consolidate the two halves, and thin the log to about ⅜" thick.

Continues ▶

8 As you continue to roll the log thinner, it will extend at each end beyond the pencil lead. If you bend the clay at the ends, you will be able to see where the lead is. Trim off the excess clay at intervals as you roll to stop the log from becoming too unmanageable. You can use a tile to smooth the log as it was used for the pen project (Pearl-a-Pen) on page 143.

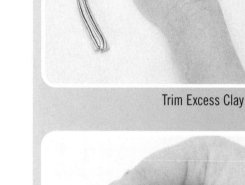

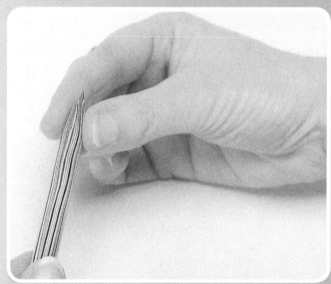

Trim Excess Clay

9 When the pencil is the desired thickness all along its length, trim the end covering the pointed lead until you can see the lead. Pinch this end into a point.

Pinch End

10 Use your knife to "sharpen" the clay at the pointed end. After baking, this will make the first sharpening easier.

Sharpen Writing End with Knife

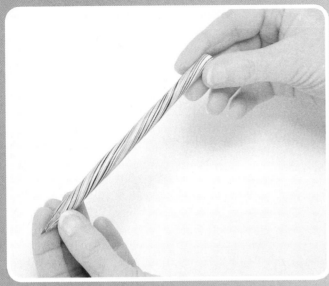

Twist to Form Spiral

11 Trim the unsharpened end of the pencil about ½" beyond the end of the lead (locate it within the clay as before, by bending the clay). Make sure that the clay at this end is sealed, or the lead will be pushed out of the clay when you write.

12 Gently twist the clay around the pencil so that the marbled lines form a spiral pattern.

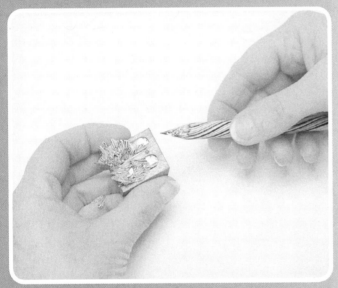

Bake and Sharpen Pencil

13 Bake the pencil for thirty minutes to be sure that the clay stays strong. While the clay is still warm, sharpen the pencil into a neat point with the pencil sharpener.

Pen Sling

Tired of never having a pen within reach? Both fun and practical, this whimsical pen begs to be returned to its matching home. With its combination of wire and clay, this refillable writing tool can be relied on for the years to come.

Must-Haves: Materials

Polymer clay: 1 block—black, turquoise; 2 blocks—purple, white • Craft knife • Pasta machine (or use a roller and wooden strips) • Ballpoint pen (BicStick pens don't melt) • Needle-nose pliers • Ball-tip stylus • Knitting needle • Superglue • One 5mm flat-back crystal • Tweezers • Ten 3mm clear flat-back crystals • 34" purple plastic-coated 18-gauge wire • Epoxy • Lipstick tube, ³/₄" in diameter • Wire cutters • Toothpicks

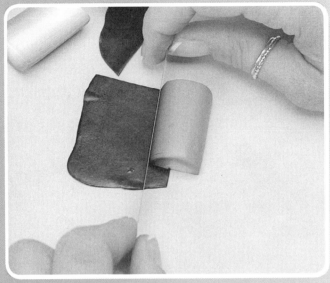

Slice Skinner Blend Cane in Half

1 Create a white and turquoise Skinner Blend cane (follow instructions on page 17 for how to make a Skinner Blend cane).

2 Cut 1½" from the cane and stand it on its end. Cut the cane in half. Roll a large ball of black clay through the fifth-largest setting of the pasta machine (or use a roller and wooden strips). Cut a straight edge along one side of the black clay with a clay blade.

3 Lay one piece of the cane halfway over the straight edge of the black clay sheet. Trim the excess black clay away from the bottom and sides of the half cane.

Wrap Combined Halves

4 Press the two halves of the cut cane (with the black strip sandwiched in between) back together. Roll ¼ block of black clay through the fourth-largest setting of the pasta machine. Wrap this clay around the entire cane. Trim any excess clay.

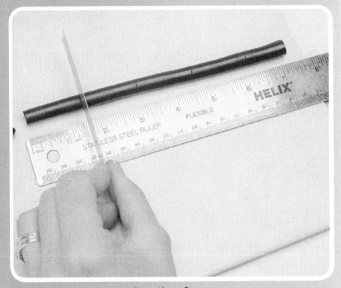

Lengthen Cane

5 Cut a ½" piece from this cane and set it aside. Roll and reduce the remaining cane to 9" long. Trim off the distorted ends and cut five 1½" sections from the 9" cane.

Continues

6 Roll ¼ block of white clay into a log the same diameter as the five cane sections. Cut the white log to 1½" long.

7 Wrap the white log in black clay that has been rolled through the fourth-largest setting of the pasta machine. Save the excess for later.

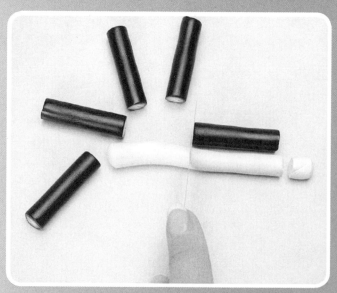

Create White Log

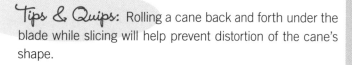

Tips & Quips: Rolling a cane back and forth under the blade while slicing will help prevent distortion of the cane's shape.

8 Place the five cane sections around the wrapped white center to form the flower. The center vein in each petal should be pointing outward from the white center. Check both sides of the flower cane to be sure that the petals are properly aligned.

Create Flower Cane

9 Blend one block of white and ¼ block of purple to make lavender clay. Roll a 1" ball of lavender clay into a snake ¼" in diameter. Pinch the top of the log along the length between your thumb and index finger to form a triangle.

Create Lavender Triangular Log

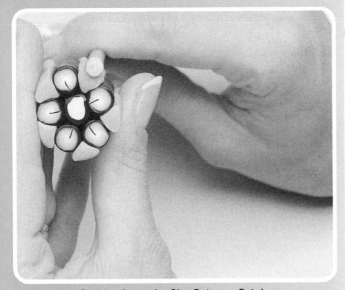

Position Lavender Clay Between Petals

10 Cut the lavender snake into five 1½" sections. Tightly pack the lavender clay into the flower cane by pressing down on each section with the handle of your needle tool. Roll the remaining lavender clay through the third-largest setting of the pasta machine. Wrap the flower cane in the lavender clay.

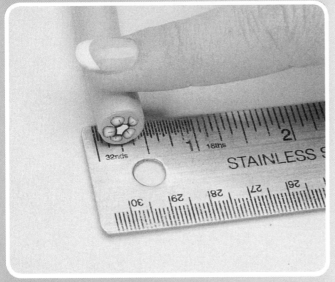

Reduce Diameter of Flower Cane

11 Cut a 1" section of the flower cane. Reduce the cane to ⅜" in diameter. Allow the cane to rest or freeze for fifteen minutes before using.

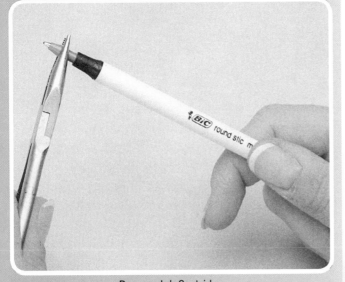

Remove Ink Cartridge

12 Carefully remove the ink cartridge from the pen by twisting and then pulling with the needle-nose pliers. Set the ink cartridge aside.

Continues

13 Roll the remaining lavender clay into a 5" log. Run the log through the pasta machine on the third-largest setting. Wrap the pen barrel in the lavender clay sheet. Trim any excess clay from the top and bottom of the pen. Roll the clay-covered barrel against your work surface with the palm of your hand to blend the seam together.

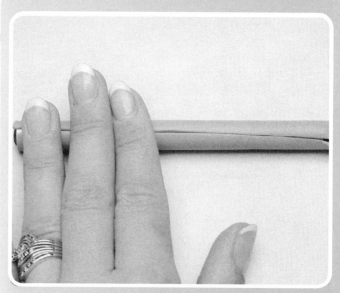

Cover Pen Barrel with Lavender Clay

14 Slice several dozen $\frac{1}{16}$" thick slices from the reduced flower cane. Lay the slices randomly over the lavender clay-covered pen barrel. Roll the pen against your work surface again until the cane slices blend into the lavender clay base. Trim any excess clay from the top and bottom of the pen barrel with a craft knife.

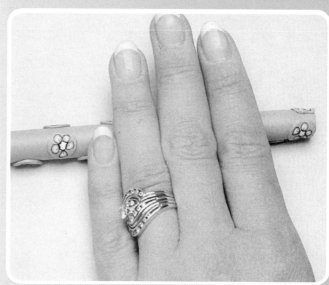

Add Cane Slices to Pen Barrel

15 Impress the surface of the lavender clay with the small end of a ball-tip stylus.

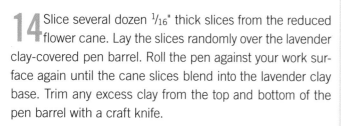

Tips & Quips: The pen will be easier to handle while texturing if placed on a knitting needle.

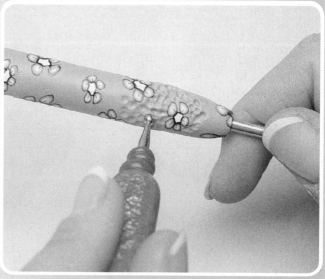

Impress Pen Barrel

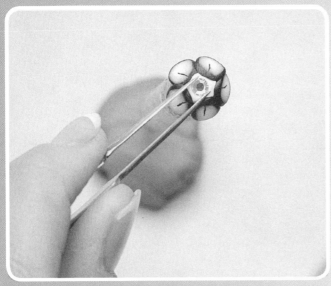

Add Flower to Top of Pen

15 Smooth the clay at the top of the pen and superglue a flattened ball of white clay to it. Reduce the leftover petal cane from Step 7 to $^3/_8$" in diameter. Slice five thin slices from the cane and superglue around the outer edge of the white clay ball to make a flower. The center veins should be facing outward from the white center.

16 Press a 5mm crystal into the white clay using the handle of the tweezers. Bake the pen on an index card at 270°F for thirty minutes.

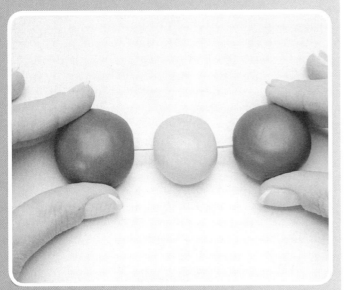

Create Base of Stand

17 Roll two $1^1/_2$" balls of purple clay and one 1" ball of lavender clay. Slightly flatten each ball by pressing with the palm of your hand against the work surface.

18 Insert two toothpicks directly opposite one another halfway into the lavender clay ball. Press the purple clay balls onto the exposed ends of the toothpicks, connecting all three balls.

Add Dots to Lavender Ball

19 Roll a small ball of black clay into a log $^1/_8$" in diameter. Cut about twenty $^1/_8$" sections from the log. Roll them into tiny balls. Press the balls randomly over the surface of the lavender ball. Flatten these balls with your fingertips.

Continues

20 Roll a tiny ball of white clay into a log $\frac{1}{16}$" in diameter. Cut twenty $\frac{1}{16}$" sections. Roll these sections into balls.

21 Press the white balls over the flattened black clay balls. Press the small end of the ball-tip stylus into the center of each white ball.

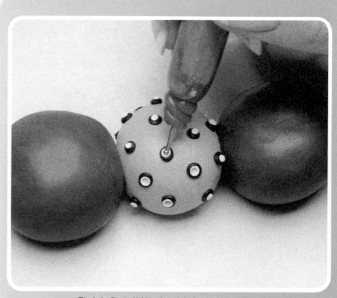

Finish Detail Work with Lavender Ball

22 Roll two $\frac{3}{8}$" balls of white clay. Press each ball over the top-center of each purple clay ball. Slightly flatten these with your fingers.

23 Cut ten $\frac{1}{8}$" slices from the large petal cane section set aside in Step 5. Place five cane slices around each of the white balls on the purple clay. The center veins should be pointing outward.

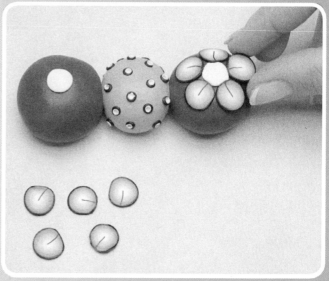

Add Flowers to Purple Balls

24 Bend $\frac{1}{2}$" at one end of the 36" purple coated wire at a 90-degree angle to form a tail. Starting right after the tail, wrap the wire around the handle of the needle tool seven times.

25 Remove the needle tool and wrap the next section of wire around a $\frac{3}{4}$" diameter lipstick tube six times. Wrap the remaining wire around the needle tool handle seven more times.

26 Remove the needle tool. Trim any remaining wire to $\frac{1}{2}$" with the wire cutters. Bend the last $\frac{1}{2}$" of wire to form another tail.

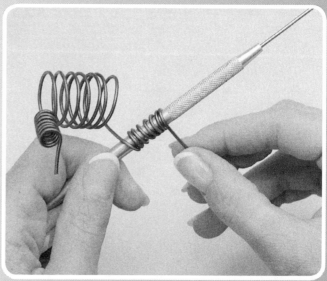

Coil Wire for Stand

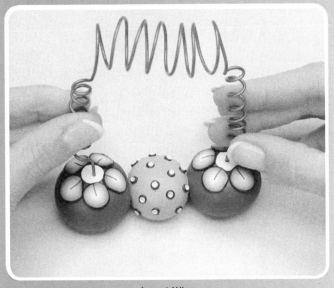

Insert Wire

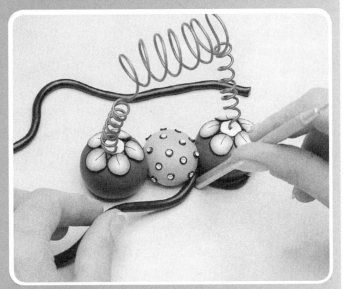

Add Finishing Touches

27 Bend the tails on both wire ends so that they face downward from the small coils. Insert a tail into the center of each flower on the stand. The wire may sit crookedly. You can adjust it after baking.

28 Roll ¼ block of black clay into a log ¼" in diameter. Wrap the log around the base of the stand. Cut off any excess clay. Blend the seam in the border together with your fingertips.

29 Bake at 270°F for one hour. When the stand is completely cool, carefully pull the wire out. Mix epoxy and insert it into the holes with a toothpick.

30 Insert the coiled wire into the glued holes. Let the glue set fifteen to twenty minutes. Bend the wire to adjust if needed.

Hearty Wire Holder

Don't feel like tacking pictures to the wall or to a bulletin board? Sick of boxy frames? Have no fear! Wire holders are here! Keep pictures of friends and family handy in these adorable stands.

Must-Haves: Materials

Polymer clay, 1 block: blue pearl, white, copper • Clay blade • Ball-tip stylus • 4' blue plastic-coated 18-gauge wire • Wire cutters • Needle tool • Epoxy

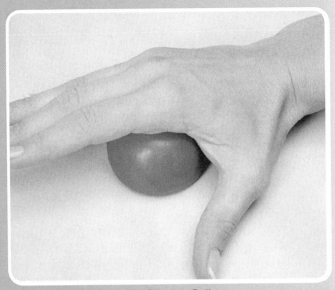

Roll Clay into Ball

1 Roll a block of blue pearl clay into a ball. Cup the palm of your hand and place it over the ball, slightly flattening it against the work surface.

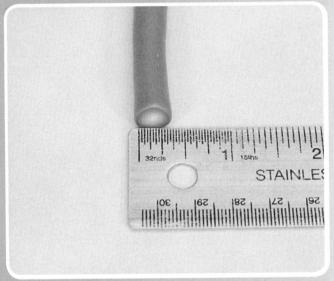

Create Skinner Blend Cane

2 Create a white and copper Skinner Blend cane (see page 17 to learn more about the Skinner Blend cane). Cut and reduce one half to ³⁄₈" in diameter.

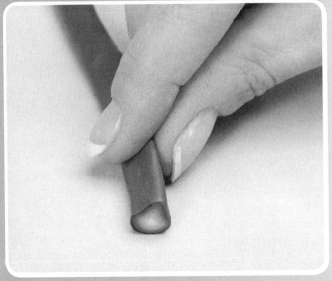

Pinch Reduced Cane

3 Between your thumb and index finger, pinch the reduced cane along its length to form a teardrop shape.

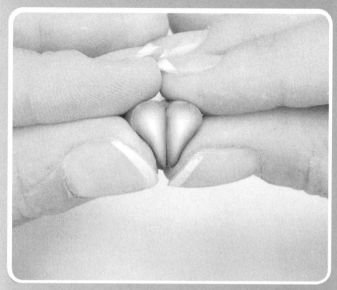

Form Hearts

4 Trim away the ends and cut the cane in half. Press the two cane sections together, pointed ends down. Let the cane rest or freeze for fifteen minutes.

5 Slice sixteen $^{1}/_{16}$" thick slices from the heart cane with a clay blade.

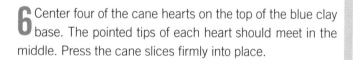

6 Center four of the cane hearts on the top of the blue clay base. The pointed tips of each heart should meet in the middle. Press the cane slices firmly into place.

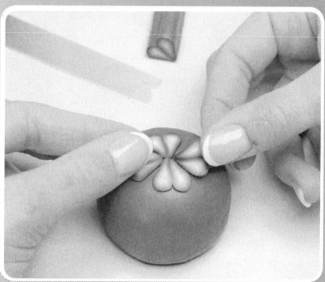

Center Four Cane Hearts on Top of Base

7 Press four more cane slices (pointed ends down) directly opposite the four hearts on the top of the base.

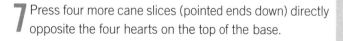

Add Four More Cane Slices to the Design

Cut Overhanging Tips of Hearts Flush with Bottom

8 Press the next four cane slices between and slightly below the first row of four hearts. Press the last four cane slices between and slightly below the second row of hearts. Cut the overhanging tips of the cane hearts flush with the bottom of the holder base.

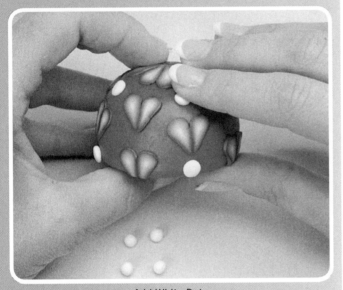

Add White Dots

9 Roll ⅛ block of white clay into a log ¼" in diameter. Cut nine ⅛" sections from the log and roll into balls.

10 Press eight of the white balls over the top and bottom of the hearts in the second row. Make sure each ball is centered between the hearts, leaving blue clay showing around each dot.

Indent Center of Dots

11 Indent the center of each white clay ball with the small end of a ball-tip stylus. Press the final dot in the center of the top four joined hearts and impress with the stylus. This center dot, along with the two on either side, will anchor the wire for the holder.

12 Cut the blue coated wire into two 12" sections and one 18" section with wire cutters. Form a tail by bending the last ¹/₂" of the end of the wire. Then wrap the wire around the handle of a needle tool eight times.

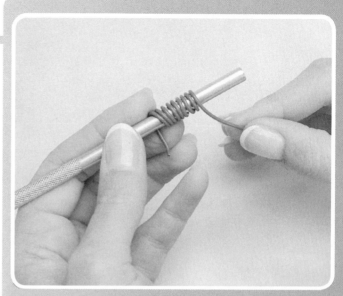

Coil Wire

13 Bend the remaining wire into a heart, as shown in the photo. Finish the end by wrapping it around the base of the wire heart three or four times to secure. Repeat this step with two 12" sections of wire, coiling the wire around the needle tool three times.

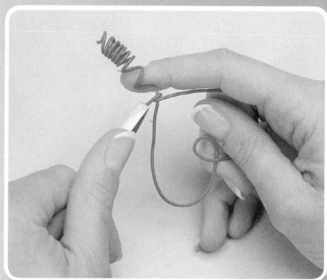

Create Wire Hearts

14 Pull the coils slightly apart and bend the wire tails so that they point downward from the coils. Insert the large wire heart into the white center dot at the top of the base. Insert the two smaller wire hearts into white dots on either side of the center ball.

15 Bake at 270°F for one hour. Allow the baked holder to cool before adjusting the wires and adding the photos. To strengthen the holder, carefully pull the wires out of the cooled photo holder and reinsert with a bit of epoxy applied to the ends.

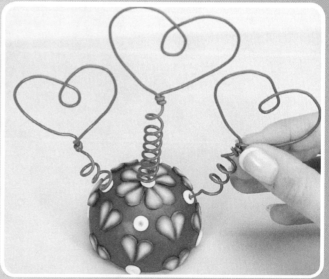

Add Finishing Touches

Pearl-a-Pen

Polymer clay-covered pens are quite popular, but this is a new, improved version of the project! The entire barrel of the pen is made with polymer clay so there is no need to worry whether a plastic barrel will survive. The ballpoint insert can be replaced when the pen runs out of ink.

Must-Haves: Materials

1 2-ounce block of black polymer clay • Ballpoint pen insert • Double-ended knitting needle, about ⅛" (3mm) thick • Tile (optional) • Tissue blade • Tools ranging in thickness for grooving: paintbrush handle, kebab skewer, piece of thick cardstock, etc. • Gold and silver pearlescent powders • Paintbrush • Pliers • Superglue • Gloss varnish • Tacky glue

Tips & Quips: Use the insert of an ordinary ballpoint pen. An inexpensive plastic pen is a good example—the inserts have a simple metal ballpoint tip attached to a tube of flexible plastic containing the ink. You can usually remove the insert by pulling off the end of the pen. Choose a knitting needle that is a little wider than the pen insert.

1 Form a 1½" ball of black clay and roll it on your work surface to make a short cylinder. Stand this on one end and pierce down through the center with the knitting needle.

2 Push the knitting needle through the clay so that the cylinder is in the center of the needle.

Create Short Cylinder

3 Lay the knitting needle down on your work surface and roll it back and forth with your fingers as though you were forming a log. The clay will thin and lengthen along the knitting needle. Keep rolling until it is about ³⁄₈" thick, or until it has reached the desired thickness.

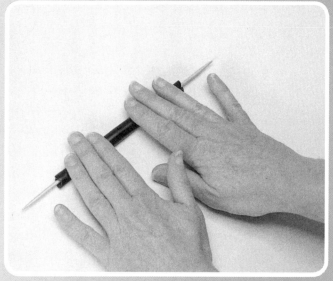

Roll out Clay Cylinder

4 To make sure that the pen body sides are really straight and smooth, roll the clay back and forth a few times with the flat surface of a tile. If you find that the clay is pulling away from the needle, squeeze the clay all along its length and then continue rolling. The pen body should be able to turn slightly on the needle, but the hole around the needle should not be too large.

Smooth Pen's Body

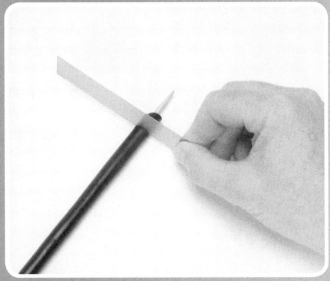

Trim End

5 With the pen body still on the needle (needle is not removed until after baking), trim one end with your blade by pressing it onto the clay while you rotate the pen. You will find you can cut neatly around the body.

Groove Pen's Body

6 Starting at the trimmed end, "groove" the clay: Hold a kebab skewer onto the clay surface at right angles to the pen and press down as you push the handle back and forth. This will rotate the clay body and the pressure will make an even groove all around. The tools used to groove the clay in the photograph are placed next to the various grooves they have made: a kebab skewer, the old pen body, and a paintbrush handle. You can make single grooves or groups of them to vary the design as desired.

Determine Correct Length

7 Lay the pen insert alongside your grooved pen body so you can see how long the pen needs to be. Cut the pen body so that it is about ¼" shorter than the insert. The ball-point tip of the insert will need to protrude out of the pen body after assembly.

Continues

8 Pinch the ballpoint end of the pen into a gently curved point around the knitting needle. Check the length and trim the other end again if necessary.

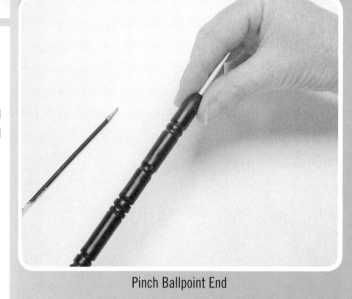

Pinch Ballpoint End

9 Form a $3/8$" ball of black clay and press it down onto a tile with the flat pad of your finger to make a disk about $1/2$" across.

10 Form a $5/16$" ball of black clay and press this onto the disk, flattening it slightly.

11 Press a $1/4$" ball onto the top. Leave this on the tile for baking.

Make Pen End

12 Hold the pen by the knitting needle and brush it all over with bands of gold and silver powders. Brush the pen end in the same way. The underlying black clay will make the powders look really rich.

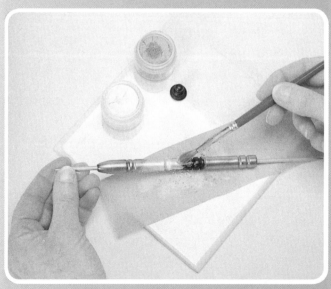

Apply Powders

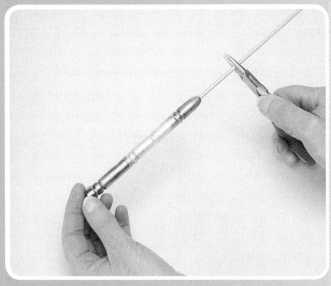

Bake and Remove Needle

13 Bake the pen and pen end for thirty minutes. When the pen is still warm but cool enough to handle, gently ease the knitting needle out of the clay. You may find it easier to grip the knitting needle with pliers as you do this.

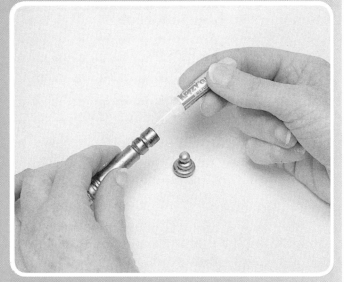

Attach Pen End and Varnish

14 Attach pen end with superglue. Varnish the pen and pen end to protect the powder.

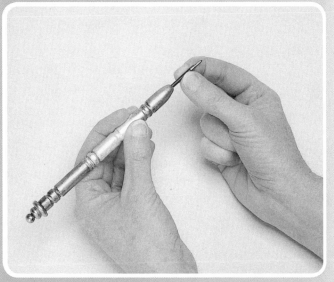

Insert Ballpoint Pen

15 Push the ballpoint pen insert into the pen body to check that it is the right length. You can cut off the end of the insert if it is too long.

16 Push the insert into the pen body as far as it will go. The tip should protrude about $1/4$" from the end. The insert should stay in by itself, but if it is loose, use a little tacky glue around the tip to hold it in place. When the pen runs out, you can replace the insert by pulling it out with pliers and inserting a new one.

Resources

Above the Mark
P.O. Box 8307
Woodland, CA 95776
Phone: (530) 666-6648
www.abovethemark.com

Accent Import-Export, Inc.
1501 Loveridge Rd., Unit 3C, Box 16
Pittsburg, CA 94565
Phone: (800) 989-2889
www.fimozone.com

American Art Clay Co., Inc. (AMACO)
6060 Guion Rd.
Indianapolis, IN 46222-2598
Phone: (800) 374-1600
www.amaco.com

American Art Stamp
3870 Del Amo Blvd. Ste 501
Torrance, CA 90503
Phone: (310) 371-6793
www.americanartstamp.com

Artistic Wire
1210 Harrison Ave.
La Grange Park, IL 60526
Phone: (630) 530-7567
www.artisticwire.com

Asian Image
800 Grant St.
San Francisco, CA 94108
Phone: (415) 398-2602
www.asianimagesf.com

Beads Plus
4750 W. Sahara Ave., Ste. 13
Las Vegas, NV 89102
Phone: (702) 259-6100
www.beadsplus.com

The Clay Factory, Inc.
P.O. Box 460598
Escondido, CA 92046-0598
Phone: (760) 741-3242
Toll Free: 1-877-Sculpey
www.Clayfactoryinc.com

Clearsnap
P.O. Boxes 98
Anacortes, WA 98221
Phone: (360) 293-6634
www.clearsnap.com

Creative Claystamps
Design Innovations
Barbara A. McGuire
P.O. Box 472334
San Francisco, CA 94147
Phone/Fax: (415) 922-6366
www.claystamp.com

Curtis Collection
8132 SE Croft Circle, A12
Hobe Sound, FL 33455
Phone: (772) 546-2846
www.curtis-collection.com

Duncan Enterprises
5673 East Shields Ave.
San Francisco, CA 93727
Phone: (559) 291-4444
www.duncanceramics.com

Hanko Designs
875 A Island Dr. #286
Alameda, CA 94502
Phone: (510) 523-5603
hankodesigns.com

Hampton Art Stamps
19 Industrial Blvd.
Medford, NY 11763
Phone: (631) 924-1335
Fax: (631) 924-1669
www.uimprint.com

Hero Arts
1343 Powell St.
Emeryville, CA 94608
Phone: (800) 822-HERO
www.herosarts.com

Hiromi Paper International
2525 Michigan Ave., #G-9
Santa Monica, CA 90404
Phone: (310) 998-0098
www.hiromipaper.com

Inkadinkado (wholesale only)
61 Holton St.
Woburn, MA 01801
Phone: (800) 888-4652
www.inkadinkado.com

Impress Me Now
Sherril Kahn
17116 Escalon Dr.
Encino, CA 91436
Phone: (818) 788-6730
www.imprssmenow.com

Judikins
17803 S. Harvard Bl.
Gardena, CA 90248
Phone: (310) 515-1115
www.judikins.com

K & Company
8500 NW River Park Dr.
Pillar 136
Parkville, MO 64152
Phone: (816) 389-4150

Kemper Enterprises
31595 12th Street
Chino, CA 91710
Phone: (800) 388-5367

Limited Edition Rubberstamps
1514 Stafford St.
Redwood City, CA 94063
Phone: (650) 299-9700
Wholesale orders: (888) STAMP-98
www.limitededitionrs.com

Magenta Rubber Stamps
3551 Blain Mont
St Hilaire
QC J3H 3B4 Canada
Phone: (450) 446-5253
www.magentarubberstamps.com

Manco Inc.
32150 Just Imagine Dr.
Avon, OH 44011-1355
Phone: (800) 321-0253
www.manco.com

National Polymer Clay Guild
Ste 115-345
1350 Beverly Rd.
McLean, VA 22101
www.npcg.org

Paintability
Delta Technical Coatings
2550 Pellissier Place
Whittier, CA 90601
Phone: (800) 423-4135
www.paintability.com

Personal Stamp Exchange
360 Sutton Pl.
Santa Rosa, CA 95407
Phone: (800) 782-6748
www.psxdesign.com

Plaid Enterprises
3225 West Tech Dr.
Norcrest, GA 30092
Phone: (678) 291-8142
Toll Free: (800) 842-4197
www.plaidonline.com

Polyform Products Co.
1901 Estes Ave.
Elk Grove Village, IL 60007
Phone: (847) 427-0020
www.sculpey.com

Polymer Clay Express
13017 Wisteria Dr., Box 275
Germantown, MD 20874
Phone: (800) 844-0138
www.polymerclayexpress.com

Postmodern Design
P.O. Box 26432
Oklahoma City, OK 73126-0432
Phone: (405) 826-0289

Prairie Craft Company
P.O. Box 209
Florissant, CO 80816-0209
Phone: (800) 779-0615
Fax: (719) 748-5112
www.prairiecraft.com

Provo Craft
151 E. 3450 North
Spanish Fork, UT 84660
Phone: (801) 794-9000
Toll Free: (800) 937-7686
www.provocraft.com

Ranger Ink
15 Park Rd.
Trinton Falls, NJ 07750
Phone: (732) 389-3535
Toll Free: (800) 244-2211
www.rangerink.com

Ready Stamp
10405 San Diego Mission Rd.
San Diego, CA 92108
Phone: (619) 282-8790
Toll Free: (877) 267-4341
www.readystamps.com

Rubber Stampede
Delta Technical Coatings
2550 Pellissier Place
Whittier, CA 90601
Phone: (800) 632-8386
www.deltacrafts.com
/RubberStampede

Rubber Stamper
P.O. Box 420
Manlapan, NJ 07726
Phone: (732) 446-4900
Toll Free: (800) 969-7176
www.rubberstamp.com

Rubber Stampmadness
P.O. Box 610
Corvallis, OR 97339
Phone: (877) 782-6762
www.rsmadness.com

Rupert, Gibbons & Spider
1147 Healdsburg Ave.
Healdsburg, CA 95448
Phone: (707) 433-9577
www.jacquardproducts.com

Speedball
2226 Speedball Rd.
Statesville, NC 28677
Phone: (704) 838-1475
www.speedballart.com

Stampers Warehouse
101 G Town & Country Dr.
Danville, CA 94526
Phone: (925) 362-9595
www.stamperswarehouse.com

Stewart Superior
2050 Farrallon Dr.
San Leandro, CA 94577
Phone: (800) 558-2875
www.stewartsuperior.com

Toybox Rubber Stamps
P.O. Box 1487
Healdsburg, CA 95448
Phone: (707) 431-1400
www.toyboxart.com

Tsukineko, Inc.
15411 NE 95th St.
Redmond, WA 98052
Phone: (800) 769-6633
www.tsukineko.com

Wee Folk Creations
18476 Natchez Avenue
Prior Lake, MN 55372
Phone: (952) 447-3828
www.weefolk.Com

Welter Stencil (customer stamp)
793 Fifth Ave.
Redwood City, CA 94063
Phone: (650) 365-2662
www.welterstencil.com

Zettiology
39570 SE Park St. #201
Snoqualmie, WA 98065
Phone: (425) 888-3191

Acknowledgments

A very special thanks to those who contributed
projects for this publication, especially:

Barbara McGuire, for the following projects:

Stamp-a-Votive, page 39

Bangle Beauty, page 60

Bead Slices, page 63

Wrist Collage, page 67

Bead Charm, page 74

Cute as a Button, page 88

Needle Cozy, page 101

Ornament-o-Stamps, page 121

Sue Heaser, for the following projects

Starry Clock, page 24

Haunted Candle Lamp, page 34

Cool Cutlery, page 43

Lovely Lampshade, page 49

Sentimental Circle, page 54

Polyclay-a-Pencil, page 126

Pearl-a-Pen, page 143

Lisa Pavelka, for the following projects:

Vintage Frame, page 30

In the Name of L-O-V-E Magnets, page 83

Perfect Pocket Album, page 96

Mr. Snowman, page 109

Pen Sling, page 130

Hearty Wire Holder, page 138

Stacey Morgan, for the following projects:

Bundle of Love, page 77

Crazy Daisy, page 91

Ball of Sun, page 106

Spring Chick, page 115

Index

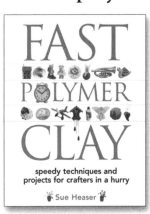
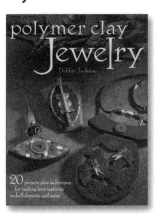
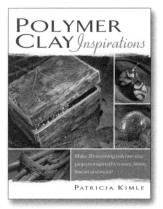

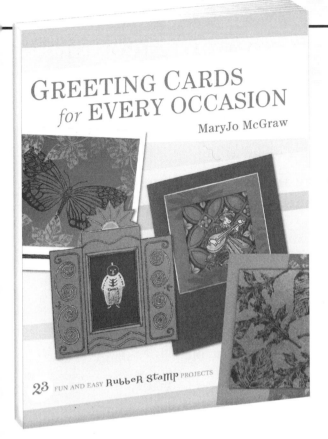

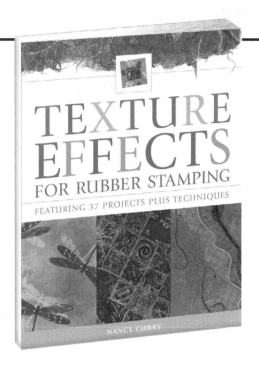

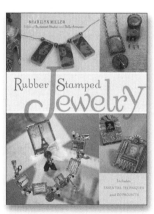
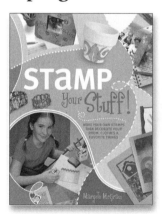